FAST

ET

First published in Great Britain in 2017 by Carcanet Press Ltd, Alliance House, 30 Cross Street, Manchester M2 7AQ www.carcanet.co.uk

First published in the USA in 2017 by HarperCollins Publishers, 10 East 53rd Street, New York, NY 10022.

A CIP catalogue record for this book is available from the British Library: ISBN 978-1-78410-470-2.

Designed by Erica Mena. Printed and bound in England by SRP Ltd.

The publisher acknowledges financial assistance from Arts Council England.

FSC
www.fsc.org

MIX
Paper from
responsible sources
FSC® C014540

Supported using public funding by
ARTS COUNCIL
ENGLAND

Also by JORIE GRAHAM

ACKNOWLEDGMENTS

Grateful acknowledgment to the editors of *The London Review of Books, The New Yorker, The Boston Review, Lana Turner, The Spectator, Folder, The Poetry Review, Poetry, The New York Times Magazine,* and *The White Review,* in which these poems first appeared.

Special gratitude to the friends who help me in so many ways: Jose Baselga, Kenneth Gold, Sol Kim Bentley, Case Kerns, Greg Whitmore, Caitlin Cook, Nancy Berger, Edward Youkilis, Tom Casey, Adam Brammer, Lila DiBiaso, Jane Miller, Tim Phillips, Michele Ciribifera, Antonella Francini, Elisa Veschini, Marco Carbonari, Bruce Guither, Tara Domaldo, Jaci Judelson, Lynn Bell, Barry Fifield, Martin Wilson, Emily Galvin, Alvaro Almanza, Bridget Read, Dan Halpern, Stephen Graham.

To my designer, Erica Mena—thank you for your gift and your forbearance.

To my family—thank you.

To Peter—for every step of the way—thank you.

for my mother and father

CONTENTS

Then the good minute goes.

Already how am I so far
Out of that minute?

—Robert Browning

I

ASHES

Manacled to a whelm. Asked the plants to give me my small identity. No, the planets.
The arcing runners, their orbit entrails waving, and a worm on a leaf, mold, bells, a
bower—everything transitioning—unfolding—emptying into a bit more life cell by

> cell in wind like this
> sound of scribbling on
> paper. I think

I am falling. I remember the earth. Loam sits
quietly, beneath me, waiting to make of us what it can, also smoke, waiting to
become a new place of origin, the other one phantasmal, trammeled with entry,
ever more entry—I spent a lifetime entering—the question of place hanging over me
year after year—me thinning but almost still here in spirit, far in, far back, behind,
privy to insect, bird, fish—are there nothing but victims—
that I could become glass—that after that we would become glacial
melt—moraine revealing wheatgrass, knotgrass, a prehistoric frozen mother's

> caress—or a finger
> about to touch

a quiet skin, to run along its dust, a fingernail worrying the edge of
air, trawling its antic perpetually imagined
end—leaping—landing at touch. A hand. On whom. A groove traversed where a god
dies. And silken before bruised. A universe *can* die. That we could ever have, or be
one body. Then picked up by the long hair
and dragged down through shaft into
being. One. Now listen for the pines, the bloom, its glittering, the wild hacking of
sea, bend in each stream, eddy of bend—listen—hear all skins raveling,
unending—hear one skin clamp down upon what now is no longer

> missing.

Here you are says a voice in the light, the trapped light. Be happy.

HONEYCOMB

Ode to Prism. Aria. Untitled. Wait. I wait. Have you found me yet. Here at my screen,
can you make me
out? Make me out. All other exits have been sealed. See me or we will both vanish.
We need emblematic subjectivities. Need targeted acquiescence. Time zones. This is
the order of the day. To be visited secretly. To be circled and canceled. I cover my
face. Total war: why am I still so invisible to you. No passport needed. If you look in,
the mirror chokes you off. No exit try again. Build bonfire. Light up screen. What are
you eating there. Can you survive on light. What is your theory of transmission. The
center holds, it holds, don't worry about that. These talkings here are not truths.
They are needs. They are purchases and invoices. They are not what shattered the
silence. Not revolutions clocks navigational tools. Have beginnings and ends.
Therefore not true. Have sign-offs. I set out again now with a new missive. Feel this:
my broken seduction. My tiny visit to the other. Busy. Temporary. In the screen
there is sea. Your fiberoptic cables line its floor. Entire. Ghost juice. The sea now
does not emit sound. It carries eternity as information. All its long floor. Clothed as
I am→in circumstance→see cell-depth→sound its atom→look into here
further→past the grains of light→the remains of the ships→starlight→what cannot
go or come back→what has mass and does not traverse distance →is all here→look
here. Near the screen there are roses. Outside a new daymoon.

Can you see my room. Inside my room. Inside me where there is room

for what I miss. I am missing all of it. It is all invisible to me. Is it invisible

to you. You have the names of my friends my markers my markets my late night

queries. Re chemo re the travel pass re where to send the photo the side effects the

distinguishing features—bot says hide—*where*—bot does not know, bot

knows, what is it to *know* here, can you hear the steps approaching, I hold my

breath here—can you hear that—bot must also hold its breath—now the steps

continue past, we can breathe freely once again, in this hiding place the visible world, among shapes and spoken words in here with my traces→can you please track me I do not feel safe→find the nearest flesh to my flesh→find the nearest rain, also passion→surveil this void→the smell of these stalks and the moisture they are drawing up→in order not to die

too fast. The die is cast. The smell of geography is here: what is the smell of chain—invisible chain—the stone on my desk I brought back from Crete, the milk I did not finish in this cup. There is smoke from the debris my neighbor burns. Don't forget to log-in my exile. This one. Female MRN 3912412. I offer myself up. For you to see. Can you not see? Why do you only see these deeds. There is a page on my desk in which first love is taking place, there is a

page on my desk in which first love is taking place again—neither of the characters yet knows they are in love—a few inches from there Mrs Ramsay speaks again—she always speaks—and Lily Briscoe moves the salt—the sky passes by rounding us— the houses have their occupants—some have women locked-in deep—see them— someone has left them in the dark—he stands next to the fridge and drinks his beer—he turns the volume up so no one hears—that is the republic—are you surveilling—we would not want you to miss the women kicked in order to abort the rape—those screams—make sure you bank them you will need them—to prove who you were when they ask—I am eating—can you taste this—it is nut butter and a mockingbird just cut short a song to fly—I tap this screen with my fork—I dream a little dream in which the fork is king—a fly lands on the screen because it is summer afternoon—locusts start up—the river here are you keeping track—I know you can see the purchases, but who is it is purchasing me→can you please track that→I want to know how much I am worth→riverpebbles how many count them exact number→and the bees that did return to the hive today→those which did not lose their way→and exactly what neural path the neurotoxin took→please track disorientation→count death→each death→very small→see it from there→count it and store→I am the temporary→but there is also the permanent→have you looked to it→for now→

DEEP WATER TRAWLING

The blades like irises turning very fast to see you completely—steel-blue then red
where the cut occurs—the cut of you—they don't want to know you they want to
own you—no—not own—we all mean to live to the end—am I human we don't
know that—just because I have this way of transmitting—call it voice—a threat—
communal actually—the pelagic midwater nets like walls closing round us—starting
in the far distance where they just look to us like distance—distance coming
closer—hear it—eliminating background—is all foreground—you in it—the only
ground—not even punishment—trawling-nets bycatch poison ghostfishing—
the coil of the listening along the very bottom—the nets weighed down with
ballast—raking the bottom looking for nothing—indiscriminate—there is nothing in
particular you want—you just want—you just want to close the
third dimension—to get something which is all—becomes all—once you are
indiscriminate—discards can reach 90% of the catch—am I—the habitat crushed
and flattened—net of your listening and my speaking we can no longer tell them
apart—the atmosphere between us turbid—no place to hide—no place to rest—you
need to rest—there is nature it is the rest—what is not hunting is illustration—not
regulated are you?—probing down to my greatest depths—2000 meters and
more—despite complete darkness that surrounds me—despite my being in my
place under strong pressure—along with all my hundreds of species—detritus—
in extreme conditions—deepwater fish grow very slowly—very—
so have long life expectancy—late reproductive age—are particularly thus
vulnerable—it comes along the floor over the underwater mountains—scraping the
steep slopes—what is bycatch—hitting the wrong target—the wrong size—not
eaten—for which there is no market—banned—endangered—such as birds—
sometimes just too much—no more space on the boat—millions of tons thrown
back dead or wounded—the scars on the seabed—the mouth the size of a football
field—and if there is no one there there is still ghostfishing—nets abandoned in the
sea they continue through the centuries to catch—mammals fish shellfish—we die
of exhaustion or suffocation—the synthetic materials last forever

Ask us anything. How deep is the sea. You couldn't go down

there. Pressure would crush you. Light disappears at 6000 feet. Ask another question: Can you hear me? No. Who are you. I am.

Did you ever kill a fish. I was once but now I am

human. I have imagination. I want to love. I have self-interest. Things

are not me. Do you have another question. I am haunted but by what?

Human supremacy? The work of humiliation. The pungency of the pesticide.

What else? The hammer that comes down on the head. Knocks the eyes out.

I was very lucky. The end of the world had already occurred. How long ago

was that. I don't know. It is not a function of knowledge. It is in a special sense

that the world ends. You have to keep living. You have to make it not become

waiting. Nothing is disturbingly visible. Only the outside continues but it

continues. So you have to find the way to make the inside

continue. Your entity is fragile. You are an object you own. At least

you were given it to own. You have to figure out what ownership

is. You thought you knew. You were wrong. It was wrong. There was

wrongness in the mix. It turns out you are a first impression. Years go

by. Imagine that. And there is still a speaker. There will always be a speaker. In the

hypoxic zones is almost no more oxygen→then there is→no more→oxygen→for real→
picture that says the speaker→who are you→where are you→going down into the dead
zones→water not water→the deeper you go he says the→scarier it gets→because
there's→nothing there→there are no→fish→no organisms→alive→no→no life→so it's *just
us*→dead zones→bigger than the Sahara he says→the largest lifeless spaces this side of the
moon→he says→she says→who is this speaking to me→I am the upwelling→I am the
disappearing→hold on→just a minute please→hold on→there is a call for you

SELF PORTRAIT AT THREE DEGREES

Teasing out the possible linkages I—no you—who noticed—if the world—no—
the world if—take plankton—I feel I cannot love anymore—take plankton—that
love is reserved for an other kind of existence—take plankton—that such an
existence is a form of porn now—no—what am I saying—take plankton—it
is the most important plant on earth—think love—composes at least half
the biosphere's entire primary production—love this—love what—I am saying
you have no choice—that's more than all the land plants on the whole planet put
together—blooms so large they can be photographed from space—everything
living—take it—here you take it, I can't hold it anymore—you don't want it—I
don't care—you carry it for now—I need to catch my breath—I want to lie here
and listen—within 50 years if we are lucky—I am writing this in 2015—like
spraying weedkiller over all the world's vegetation—that's our raw
material, our inventory, right now, we are going through the forms of worship,
we call it news, we will make ourselves customers, we won't wait, how fast can we be
delivered—will get that information to you—requires further study—look
that's where the river used to be—one morning I woke up and I was born—I

realized I was born—earth was the place to be—hurtling winding unwinding thick
nexus looking up at sky down at soil will I learn how to stand on it—I will—I am
standing, look, I am a growth possibility, will accumulate a backlog, will become
an informed consumer→shapeless unspendable future→this was my song to you→
I stood for the first time on my own→unimaginable strength in these feet, these
hands→what am I supposed to not harm→I want to touch things till they break→that
is how to see them→all the points of contact→entropy, diminishment, pressing
and then pulling back and looking, leaving alone→unimaginable→a meaning in
every step→I change shape→it is allowed→wind proves everything wrong→so
nothing is unimagined→press too far and there you have it→dream→shape of

certainty→wide forces gathering in the sunlight→thought→feel this it is
serenity→this is completeness→something darted into the bush→no forcing
just curve flight gathering terror unfinality clumps of feel/think then tree swallows
bursting up out of the tree they were not leaves after all the field of rules not visible but
suddenness its own rule→surprise. Not chaos. If I listen: everything: chant of.

Dwell there. Crosshatchings of me and emptiness. Seeing into. Falls here. Given
definition. Define anthropos. Define human. Where do you find yourself. Is it
worth waiting around for. Wind. Bring your brain along. Flesh too, has to be
married off. And your smile. Silly damaged. Don't even think about it. We are all
tired. We need the tools to make the tools. Also the headdress. Are we ahead of
time or too late? No one is noticing us the whistle blows the birds don't do
any damage. Dwell.

SHROUD

I wrote you but what I couldn't say→we are in systemicide→it would be good to be frugal→it is impossible not to hunger for eternity→here on the sand watching the sandstorm approach→remembering the so-called archaic→and the blossoming of→feeling the→gambling in our blood like a fold and its sheet of→immaculate→its immaculate sheet→I saw the holy shroud once did you→we leave a lot of stain→we are wrapped and wrapped in gossamer days→at the end what is left is a trail→of bodyfluid→of all this fear→can you feel

it→it beats under my shroud→I have to stop the lullaby→when questioned said yes→said I almost believe you are there→you are there→said the season of periods is over→said hold each of us up to the light after our piece of time is cut off we are the long ribbon of our days nothing more→do you mind→and a crowd comes and looks at the long worm of our bodytrace→in this light→they will see the stainage of our having lived and think it has a shape→it is dirt→it is ooze's high requiem→becoming→soaked with ancestors→and country→one small leopard carried on the mare→and the fluid comes→comes from the cavities→in a few of the lives that stain will be worshiped→just look→the wide light-reflecting light-returning ribbon of one man's days on earth will make the individuals in the crowd who are so blessed as by live virus feel they can be healed. And some of them will be.

   The pain you undergo can do that for another. If you gave your life by living it.

In such a way as to leave a trace. To another who goes home to her small kitchen all will

be different. From this moment forward. I will change I am changed. I have seen what the

minutes are, they were held up for me in front of the cathedral, have seen with my own eyes

what the days are, have seen what this cup is when I pour the milk into it, have seen in the

passage between cup and lip the secret I now carry in to you, in the other room, in your

highchair, your wheelchair, can bring time into you right from this cup, can bring the passage

of new time in through the new love I have filtered into the pouring. It is not that I

can read between the lines there are no lines. It is not that we will ever meet again or that the chip in everything we touch is forgotten. It is not that I have forgotten that the sensors

are watching the x-rays the mesh the bird of paradise. Now he slides out a twenty. Now the

fireworks go off

                    by mistake too soon. When asked if she had anything to declare. And they took
it from her anyway. It was her name. It quivered leaving. It turns out she was ok without. So
then one is posthumous. How can I find myself again. In this world. I want to in *this* world.
Don't give me the apparition in the air. It is positively marvelous. When are you going to tell
me what is going on. It is going on. The calculations are off. Something was too long. Some
years had to be cut off. It all had to fit. Who is this talking now. The rear view talks a lot. Too
loud. I can't explain it now, will later on. Trust me. Why. Because I made it with my hands.
I made it all with these hands. It is not personal. So you have to hurry up. Or you will not bear
it, will not. How many lights they must see going on now as it is planet earth and we still

have some fuel left for these nights as they come on→
                                        and we tip over to enter into the circle
light makes→me with this cup of milk→as there is nothing else to give you→the water is not
safe→on the way home I saw mushrooms pushing up through roots→I wish to belong to the
earth as they do→saw an abandoned tugboat on the hillside and some trees still carrying their
colors→wild yellows and reds→as if they were trying to indicate this could still be called
home→in a corner a piece of marble from→grain from→grease someone had shipped here
at great expense from→and I thought about that word *expense*→and sympathy like a baby animal
leaning into the sound of words because I had vocal cords→and they asked for that→and
something was down there in me I myself barely owned→but which truly thrilled if a
word was uttered→and I got it right→and how it was ready to declare ownership
over each thing it thought→as if each time the assignment were new→and the visible world
each morning beginning again to dig into my face to→declare me the owner of my
minutes→and what was I going to do with them outside of surviving→having come down to
surviving→as the vague memory of the world you are living in now came to me→down from
what my mind thought→trying to summon the idea of duty→once I heard someone say very
loudly from a podium→the system is broken we need to fix the system→we need to fix the
system the system is broken→and how he spoke of the love of people→and how
unfortunately we could not be omnipresent sitting here today watching you drink the
milk→and remembering the sprouts of tall bright grass growing around the podium→
and how what we saw was their having been pushed aside by its placement there→

I miss the toolbar I miss the menu I miss the place where one could push delete

from THE ENMESHMENTS

Still more terrible the situation. I do not want the 3D glasses, friend, it's all already 3D.
Look up look out. *Out*—what is that. Will you come out? Can you? Why don't you try. Still
more terrible. A veil of haze. A haze of years. The dancers still there. Who are those
others? Those are people. People made from a file. Someone printed them. It's additive.
But what if I only want to subtract. It's too abstract. I have no contract. Cannot enact impact
interact. Look: the mirrored eye of the fly, so matter of fact. Hot tears yes but not in
retrospect. Flagstones after rain my very own dialect. No do not want the 3D glasses, friend,
it is already all

correct→sun-baked→do not need 3D to resurrect→just look up look
out. *Out*. Can you come out? Why don't you try. You *can* make you *you*. It starts with want.
Hereby multiplied, commodified→you such a one→created by successive layers laid down
till→(push *print*)→the thing's→created→slick→entire→it has to be entirely new→
once started you cannot be modified→you have been simplified→singularized→oh look the
damselfly→can it land (no) on each of these wafer-thin strata→horsefly firefly dragonfly→
hoverfly→on the gladioli→ranunculi→sandfly mayfly→(quiet)→housefly→oh objecti-
fied→thinly sliced stratified fortified horizontal cross-section of the eventual→unified→till
all traces of the layers are erased→prettified→creating the sensation of a single solid

ground→emulsified→petrified→gradations stations seams→such as
the world. Or time. Sintering, fusing. Such that the thing before you appears whole. Is whole. ·
Also holy. As in stereolithography. Your friend will be made for you—yr apostrophe—will be
all yours→the high-power fusion of→small particles of→plastic, ceramic, metal, glass→
powdery→sturdy→provided with life→in custody→a series of layers→consecrations→
make its acquaintance→world face to face→will be seen for some time→for your time→your
truism→awesome→*must be said with enthusiasm*→how do you do, for example→being
absolute about it→historical→the only mortal left perhaps→no way to be sure→of
the custom→earthworn threadworn→no way to be sure→among these others→even
foolish would be good→speechless→every idea paralyzed→what you *wanted*→still
more→terrible→the art of conversion of convection of

conversation—how do you do—goodbye—please—(these were the words)—please thank you I
beg your pardon I beg it not at all no I shall be delighted—I am begging—every time

we were more grateful—I could think of nothing else—what was daily life—what was my dream—two human beings—confront each other—speechless—because they can think of nothing to say …

(Spellbound by the history—of god—unknowing—I feel my theory collapsing—I say *I*—I say too early too late—the Greeks perhaps I say)—*Suhrawardi believed this leader was the true pole (quth) without whose presence the world could not continue to exist*—the world cannot continue to exist—he was attempting an act of imagination—what lies at the heart of—at the core of—truth must be sought in—the soul must be educated and informed by—the true sage in his opinion excels in—total reality stands before us as—look up look out—there is always the world—a dove drifts by with nothing to do—who is the couple down there in obscurity—they have sought out the obscurity—it is an immense system to link all the insights—truth must be found—wherever it can be found—consequently—as its name suggests—for reasons that remain obscure—I shall abjure—mon amour—are you the viewer—as such the destroyer—who are you in layers—come to take me to my playdate—my interviewer my rescuer—no—my caricature—as in here I extend my arm and you, you …

I will say "you".

WE

lost all the wars. By definition. Had small desires and fundamental fear. Gave our
children for them, paid in full, from the start of time, standard time and standard
space, with and without suspension of disbelief, hungry for the everyday, wide
awake, able to bring about a state of affairs by bodily movement, not even gradually,
not hesitating, not ever, gave brothers fathers sisters mothers. Lost every war.
Will lose the ones to come. By definition. That woman. That
ocean. Careful how you fool around. There is form and it knows the difference. Go
alone. Hold back. Transfigure. Promise. Go alone. Transfigure. Keep promise. All this
is what the wind knows. It has never lost a war. Has a notion to be almost
wordless. Has need. But not like ours. No sir it knows acceptance—strange isn't
it—so does the stream—it has a hillside—knows acquiescence—does not lose,
has no lips, does not love, does not carry on—or maybe it does, yes—but not as we
do—no generations, no forgetting—no eyes desiring what they see too
much—the blossom—the bluebird—the crease in the hillside—no too much, no
thankfulness, nothing to do, or that has to be done, nothing to forget—please let me
forget—I did not do that—it could not have been me—where shall I hide now—I
shall be found—no one can find them, the stream, the bones in the culvert,
the pigeons hovering near the steam shaft—no one can find them they need not
hide—the stones, the steel, the galaxies—shrinking or in-
                                                    creasing, no war—
nothing—nothing can see itself—nothing can think—there is no prevailing—nor
lack—just as it should be—death yes but as a gathering, energy done—not a lost
war—just a merging with what comes—with what has come before—it does not
turn around—it is not looking over its shoulder—nerveless—were we needed—as
wind was—lost all wars—even the one with time—all of the time—all of the

times. Looked for every intersection. Time and fiction. Asked can it be

true? Time and history. Asked can it really be true? This is happening. But is

not what the real feels like. The past? Is senseless. Collapse the *it-has-been*

says the wind. Look but not back. Any wind will tell you. You have not been *there*.
In the strictest sense. Are on display. There is no private space. Nothing is taking
place. It will not stick. Also

what more shall we do to others. To otherness. No,
to *others*. We are in some strange wind says the wind. Are in the enigma of
pastness. It is shedding its aircraft, its radar, it has its back against a
bodiless sorrow, the bodies are all gone from it, the purchases have all been made,
it is so extreme this taking-the-place-of, this standing-in-for, this disappearing of all
the witnesses—this is inconceivable—conceive it—the floating faces which carried
themselves as bodies through all the eras—they say nothing—nothing
that you will ever see—you are so blind—in each instant blind—the problem is
insoluble—also senseless—there is no real to which you can refer—and yet the
bodies are all in it—whatever remains—the observable witnesses to the past—this
debt—the relation of this to absolute silence—listen—it is absolutely silent back

there—from here nothing ever is to have happened—no one made you—the
streets the imperial cities the cord from father to daughter certain butterflies
certain kinds of armor plate the great highways the grease the model sitting for the
sculptor the woman she is the clay she is the destinations of the steel and oil, the
signatures, the millions of signatories to the past, the launching and relaunching of
boys men ships craft from land to sea from sea to land to air to sea to land the birds
the hidden fox the rabbits in the field as the highway is being cut the deer going
deeper into the brush the pyramids the broken columns the mice that have dug a
nest beneath—oh analogy—apprehension strikes me vastly down—we are way
past
    intimation friend—the pastness of→you can only think about it→it won't
be there for you→you can talk about it→they are gone who came before→left us
nothing but ourselves→on our tiny axis of blood→surrounded by all the broken
columns→the marble which will itself surrender→to time→to radioactivity→to
→we are all we ever were→necessary because of breeding→weak→dying→and
then there are clocks→butterflies cyclamens geometrical patterns lacerations of
space where galaxies grow→a bottle of whiskey deep in the soil no one found→it
descended→cloth with serial numbers→one says made in the USA→underneath
death it says *made in*→where shall we put the theory of reading→there never was

metaphor→action unfolded in no temporality→anticipation floods us but we never were able—not for one instant—to inhabit time→listen→the last step is this feeling you have here→just as long as we keep doing this→I write you read→a with-time-ness→an unexpected nobility→above and below flow by, cold as they are→the universals keep→solar ghosts flare→turn to cash→on this small fire the earth keep reading→I say to myself keep on→it will not be the end→not yet→my children sleep→not yet→a friend who's dead said this to me→it is not dead→

FAST

or starve. Too much. Or not enough. Or. Nothing else?
Nothing else. Too high too fast too organized too invisible.
Will we survive I ask the bot. No. To download bot be
swift—you are too backward, too despotic—to load greatly enlarge
the cycle of labor—to load abhor labor—move to the
periphery, of your body, your city, your planet—to load, degrade, immiserate,
be your own deep sleep—to load use your lips—use them
to mouthe your oath, chew it—do the
dirty thing, sing it, blown off limb or syllable, lick it back on
with your mouth—talk—talk—who is not
terrified is busy begging for water—the rise is fast—the drought
comes fast—mediate—immediate—invent, inspire, infil-
trate, instill—here's the heart of the day, the flower of time—talk—talk—

Disclaimer: bot uses a growing database of all your conversations
to learn how to talk with you. If some of you
are also bots, bot can't tell. Disclaimer:
you have no secret memories,
talking to cleverbot may provide companionship,
the active ingredient is a question,
the active ingredient is entirely natural.
Disclaimer: protect your opportunities, your information, in-
formants, whatever you made of time. You have nothing else
to give. Active ingredient: why are you
shouting? Why? Arctic wind uncontrollable, fetus
reporting for duty, fold in the waiting which recognizes you,
    recognizes the code,

the peddler in the street everyone is calling out.

Directive: report for voice. Ready yourself to be buried in voice.

It neither ascends nor descends. Inactive ingredient: the monotone.

Some are talking now about the pine tree. One assesses its

disadvantages. They are discussing it in many languages. Next

they move to roots, branches, buds, pseudo whorls, candles—

     active ingredient:

they run for their lives, lungs and all. They do not know what to do with

their will. Disclaimer: all of your minutes are being flung down.

They will never land. You will not be understood.

The deleted world spills out jittery as a compass needle with no north.

Active ingredient: the imagination of north.

Active ingredient: north spreading in all the directions.

Disclaimer: there is no restriction to growth. The canary singing in

     your mind

     is in mine. Remember:

     people are less

than kind. As a result, chatterbot is often less than kind. Still,

you will find yourself unwilling to stop.

Joan will use visual grammetry to provide facial movements.

I'm not alone. People come back

again and again. We are less kind than we think.

There is no restriction to the growth of our

cruelty. We will come to the edge of

understanding. Like being hurled down the stairs tied to

a keyboard, we will go on, unwilling to stop. The longest

real world conversation with a bot lasted

11 hours, continuous interaction. This

bodes well. We are not alone. We are looking to improve.

The priestess inhales the fumes. They come from the

mountain. *Here* and *here*. Then she gives you the machine-gun run of

syllables. Out of her mouth. Quick. You must make up your

answer as you made up your

question. Hummingbirds shriek. Bot is amazing he says, I believe it knows
the secrets of the Universe. He is more fun to speak with
than my actual living friends she says, thank you. This is the best thing
since me. I just found it yesterday.
I love it, I want to marry it.
I got sad when I had to think
that the first person
who has ever understood me
is not even it turns out
human. Because this is as good as human gets.
He just gives it to me straight. I am going to keep him
forever. I treated him like a computer
but I was wrong. Whom am I talking to—
You talk to me when I am alone. I am alone.

Each epoch dreams the one to follow.

To dwell is to leave a trace.

I am not what I asked for.

II

READING TO MY FATHER

I come back indoors at dusk-end. I come back into the room with
your now finished no-longer-aching no-longer-being
body in it, the candle beside you still lit—no other
light for now. I sit by it and look at it. Another *in*
from the one I was just peering-out towards now, over
rooftops, over the woods, first stars.
The candle burns. It is so quiet you can hear it burn.
Only I breathe. I hear that too.
Listen I say to you, forgetting. Do you hear it Dad. Listen.
What is increase. The cease of increase.
The cease of progress. What is progress.
What is going. The cease of going.
What is knowing. What is fruition.
The cease of. Cease of.
What is bloodflow. The cease of bloodflow
of increase of progress the best is over, is over-
thrown, no, the worst is yet to come, no, it is
7:58 pm, it is late Spring, it is capital's apogee, the
flow's, fruition's, going's, increase's, in creases of
matter, brainfold, cellflow, knowing's
pastime, it misfired, lifetime's only airtime—candle says
you shall *out* yourself, out-
perform yourself, grow multiform—you shall self-identify as
                                                still
mortal—here in this timestorm—this end-of-time
storm—the night comes on.

Last night came on with you still *here.*

Now I wait here. Feel *I can think.* Feel *there are no minutes in you*—

Put my minutes there, on you, as hands—touch, press,

feel the flying-away, the leaving-sticks-behind under the skin, then even the skin

abandoned now, no otherwise now, even the otherwise gone.

I lay our open book on you, where we left off. I read. I read aloud—

grove, forest, jungle, dog—the words don't grip-up into sentences for me,

it is in pieces,

I start again into the space above you—*grandeur wisdom village,*

tongue, street, wind—hornet—feeler runner rust red more—oh

more—I hear my voice—it is so raised—on you—are you—*refinery portal*

land scald difference—here comes my *you*, rising in me, my feel-

ing your *it,* my *me,* in-

creasing, elaborating, flowing, not yet released from form, not yet,

still will-formed, swarming, mis-

informed—*bridegroom of spume and vroom.*

I touch your pillowcase. I read this out to you as, in extremis, we await

those who will come to fix you—make you permanent. No more vein-hiss. A

masterpiece. My phantom

father-body—so gone—how gone. I sit. Your suit laid out. Your silver tie. Your

shirt. I don't know

what is

needed now. It's day. *Read now,* you'd say. Here it is then, one last time, the

news. I

read. *There is no*

precedent for, far exceeds the ability of, will not

adapt to, cannot

adapt to,

but not for a while yet, not yet, but not for much longer, no, much

sooner than predicted, yes, ten times, a hundred times, all evidence

points towards.

What do I tell my child.

Day has arrived and crosses out the candlelight. Here it is now the

silent summer—extinction—migration—the blue-jewel-
butterfly you loved, goodbye, the red kite, the dunnock, the crested tit, the cross-
billed spotless starling (near the top of the list)—smoky gopher—spud-
wasp—the named storms, extinct fonts, ingots, blindmole-made-
tunnels—oh your century, there in you, how it goes out—
how lonely are we aiming for—are we there
yet—the orange-bellied and golden-shouldered parrots—
I read them out into our room, I feel my fingers grip this
page, where are the men who are supposed to come for you,
most of the ecosystem's services, it says,
will easily become replaced—the soil, the roots, the webs—the organizations
of—the 3D grasses, minnows, mudflats—the virtual carapace—the simulated action of
forest, wetland, of all the living noise that keeps us
company. Company. I look at you.
Must I be this machine I am
become. This brain programming
blood function, flowing beating releasing channeling.
This one where I hold my head in my hands and the chip
slips in and *click* I go to find my in-
formation. The two-headed eagle, the
beaked snake, the feathered men walking sideways while looking
ahead, on stone, on wall, on pyramid, in
sacrifice—must I have already *become* when it is all still
happening. Behind you thin machines that ticked and hummed until just now
are off *for good*. What I wouldn't give, you had said last night, for five more
minutes here. *You can't imagine it*. Minutes ago.
Ago. It hums. It checks us now, monitoring
this minute fraction of—the MRI, the access-zone, the
aura, slot, logo, confession-
al—I feel the hissing multiplying
satellites out there I took for stars, the bedspread's weave, your *being* tucked-in—
goodnight, goodnight—*Once upon a time* I say into my air,
and I caress you now with the same touch
as I caress these keys.

THE POST HUMAN

Standing next to your body you have just gone.

How much of you has gone has it all gone all

at once.

It has been just a minute now—I don't want the time to go in this direction—it does.

Now it has been two. Elsewhere. Elsewhere someone gets on a train—

we're almost there, a man says to a child,

prepare for landing, the fields are rushing towards us,

we are setting out with the picnic, the woods seem far but we have all day …

Standing next to you, holding the hand which stiffens, am I

outside of it more than before, are you not inside?

The aluminum shines on your bedrail where the sun hits. It touches it.

The sun and the bedrail—do they touch each other more than you and I now.

Now. Is that a place now. Do you have a now.

The day stands outside all around as if it were a creature. It is natural. Am I to think

you now

natural? Earlier, is it an hour ago, you sat up briefly looked

out. Said nothing but I looked at your eyes and saw them see. You saw

the huckleberry, the plume of rose, the silver morning grow as if skinning night,

that animal, till day came out raw and bleeding.

Daybreak mended it for now. I saw you see the jay drop

into the clearing light, light arrive, direction assert itself for you—what for—but yes

that is East, with its slow grace. The jet went by way overhead.

Shade one more time under the tree you love. Shadow then shade.

Its body like a speech the tree was finally allowed to make, coming free of night.

A statement. Which would evolve as it grew to

know—[you passed in here][you left]["you"—what did your *you* do?]—the bush, the

bird, hills, the hundreds of branches like snakes, top and bottom making their event—the unbleaching from dawn to the rich interweaving

knowledges of

the collapse of knowledge

which is day.

Saw you sit up and look out. Just like that. *Information is our bread and butter*

is what you loved to say. We each have a thing we loved

to say, I think. How many minutes have passed now. Have we caught up yet with

where we just

were? There are so many copies of this minute.

Not endless but there sure are a lot

from when I started, going through my motions, part of

history—or, no, cup in hand, end at hand, trying to hide from the

final ampersand. Where are you waiting, *where out there*, the wrong part of me now

wants to

ask. And turns around and says, cue consequence, cue

occasion. There on the bed just now—(look, all of a sudden now I cannot write "your"

bed)—I watch your afterlife begin to

burn. Helpful. Making a space we had not used

before, could not. Undimmed, unconsumed. In it this daylight burns.

THE MEDIUM

Lethe—river of unmindfulness—what am I to forget now—*forget sweetheart*—and

I wake—and

again we are being hatched, the shell breaks now, just now, a crack, in time, on the

horizon line and

outside the pane across Memorial Drive the Charles is channeling scribbling erasing

itself while all along chattering self-wounding self-dividing, slowing at bank, at

streamline, at meander, then quick now trying-out scribbling again—why not—one must

keep trying

to make

the unsaid said—that is the task of the surface—rivermist rising like ectoplasm off this

downstate slate-weight silhouetted think-tank—sky's overflowing checkbook,

nonstop signatures filigreed by wintered trees—no debt unpaid—all trans-

mutation's molecules—silvergrey tulle, vestigial, lacteal, millennial—[colonial]—if

this is prophecy it's underwater, self-consuming, does not know what to do with

itself

except be carried forward—inexorably—drift into drift—not really anything like

fate—*my fear teaches me more* I think looking down at the metallic swirls, enameled,

processional, unidirectional and oh so floral although more archival now as the

crisping dawn-blue

spews itself

onto itself

anew—parts so exact they fit their own exactness—

such that nothing about themselves can escape themselves—

a complete reason reasoned or a completely collective error—oh—

completely has never meant so much to me—as I look down now at the utterly

swallowed self-swallowing river—a constant continual final word—birds

rising from its tongue—first words final words—crumbling daybreak opened up by

reedheads in wind, rattling seedpods which could be small flights from stalk to stalk,

and then above the wider-winged arriving now, creaturely, to land, here, heavily,
carefully—as further downriver there is the sea—and then there is
no more—no more crooked intervention of the singular—no more—all wide all
                                  open, no alternative
possible—as all is all again—all entered again—all action futile—but here, still
                                upriver, each bird can
                                land in its
                                own place, or take
                                off just
                                like that,
as the helicoidal flow lays-in its next braid then its next, just like that—the place for
nymphs for rivermists—every few feet a spinning which is the outcome of
some rip upstream, the origin of the like downstream, bird-landing like a blow of
fist—though nothing is felt—roiling away, recreating what needs no creating—and
all of it, all along its length, about my dream does not know
                                anything, about the
phone appointment set for 6:15—she's late—and the keys to my house sit in the
plate—and outside my shell now dawn and the breaking of it from which I
                                shall be pulled
again, pulled out, all darkness knocked like ash from the celestial cigarette of the
tired god—who hasn't seen it all—nightshift, cabaret of aftermaths, more drifting
now, some geese in it—now dawn outright—the pink beginning as the deity
inhales, takes a deep drag on it which shafts down light from a bright
break in cloud, white tunneling—and something holds its hand out
                                here and it
                                means it, is not
                                begging, not a
gentle request, also take off your
shoes your heart your skin it says, take it all off, the palm outstretched, the palm
waiting, take it, take it all now, the thing you call *you*, this chatter all around, this
roof over your head, this address—until it is time and nothing is left to
                                chance, and I
                                glance up at the
kitchen clock—is that a cellphone or birdcall I think—then there it

is—where I hear newspaper land on sill—and the phone's tone
rings, and Patricia-Michele, unknown to me, area
                                        code 304, is already
                                        letting in
the exit, tired, all the once-born seeking refuge again I think as
egged on by them she speaks to me, fast, most agile, my father wishes immediately
                                        for me to know it
is him, he is so well, has a new body, has moved fast through the
                                        book of life,
I will understand when I come there, should not be afraid, nothing useless is re-
called, the voice which is his which is hers so firm, full of urgent finishings,
orders, find this, protect that, but mostly how sweet the ending was which had
to us appeared so sick the body so invaded left to die full of moaning that would not
stop—curled up—fists gripped—and terror if medicine not given now, right now,
and leave the vial nearby, want to see it, make sure there is
                                        enough, ask the doctor
                                        again if more
                                        can be taken—
all not-sailing at dawn but moored too deep in
shallow harbor, stuck, keel of pain, sea gone, him in stony shallows,
cold, the blanket pulled up by his good hand again, again, as if to bring the
                                        water up but it
recedes, the nakedness is all exposed, it is becoming more, the bones are
coming up and you, mouthing the air looking for air, the room around
your mouth now seeking breath fast-growing emptier, vast, as all the books stare
                                        down at us, the
ink, the whiteness of the paper in its place, awaiting use, everything awaiting
use, your whispers hoarse wandering through thickets of walls,
the labyrinths of rooms that were a home—what is it pulverizes you—what is it
pulverizes rooms that made all the sense in the world to us as we walked in and
through eyeing each place we living know—even the secrets are assigned, are
pulverized—all this round where tomorrow there will be candles burning when
they wash you, dress that body, lay it out—the hand meant for tearing

and pointing turned like a shucked shell with no palm to hold a thing again—a
coin would slip through—the boots in the corner seem to have

                                     your feet in them—
what is this fat dimension you forfeit—what dimension are you becoming,

                                     have you
become—her saying now you say *we can wander*, or is it *wonder* she is saying

                                   and that *we do*

                                   not need to

                                   know—
but what made you shake so, what did you seem to greet increasingly, gently,
again and again, each day more, sometimes near noon sometimes evenings as if

                                   entering

                                   some far
classroom, a face, a person on a street approaching you, the years of lifetime
closing, sometimes your hand soaring as if conducting an
anger a burning—rejecting then inviting destruction—
and when I wheeled you to the window in the morning to look out—look out I said,
look Dad it's Spring, look in the distance—here it comes—that was not what

                                   you saw,
not that phantom coming again over the hills, no,
that beggar coming to sell you another year and at what cost, no
you said, no, that is not what is coming—and you would not look out
at the light striking the one far field in the distance brighter, spring-wheat just

                                   starting up, glistering, no

                                   truck for
the treasure of the beam pointing out *this* rather than *that*—*this* tree
that roof, *this* rich man's field of soy, not that one's final bales—although they were
gold in the day and would feed the herd. No.
Some other invitation you had not requested glimmered.
Your eyes floated above the drift of our kind's love-shimmer.
How sweet you were then, now that you speak of it to me from such distance,
to let us murmur and caress and rub your hands as if our hands were prayers.
Ointments for the chapping. Astringents. Disinfectants. The bag

changed and changed as soon as you swallowed—all passing

through you and out. Nothing staying in. No *in*.

No great wisdoms now, they do not interest you.

The time for wisdom is past you tell me she says, it is not useful.

But to tell mother to be careful when she comes and not be afraid.

That she will find her people, you in particular, waiting—

just not right away—and again you repeat it—not right away—

tell her not to be afraid when she comes which is not right away

because at first she will be alone.

She will finish her business and let go of the stories. The stories are an

impediment. You must be in them now, you tell me, but they are all string and

knot, they catch you up—spilled blood—the love—the car is

pushed—the time is right—your symbol, your scene, your out-

come—how I wish I could pull you free, you say, there is above just right there

above

this music—can you not hear—not see (*can not* says Patricia-Michele to

you as you are her whom is she speaking to)—(*no she can not*)—can he hear

me I ask—*of course*—are you ok I ask—oh he is laughing she says

at your question—it was so beautiful he says thank you you took such

care the passage was a lovely path—and I look at the room—we have cleaned

it up—we have changed the place—the bed has been moved—

what is this number I have called—I give my credit card—I wanted to know

you are all right—there is language—there are the appalling fields—

there is long ago—I am all past—it is all past—how did you

get out—do we ever get out—the time is up it

seems, he has rejoined the others he is saying goodbye be careful of

strangers or a stranger I cannot hear it right, I give my credit card, 0057 5532 0736

5118, expiration date 4/18—security code?—we shall have to bill you for the full

two hours she says, although it's not her anymore, or is *just* her. Is that understood?

And I am at the window again. And down there below me again the riversurface

stares. It is all even now. It glints and gleams in tidy rows and rolls and dents of

wind. The day is

long. It flirts with nothingness. It always does.

VIGIL

Again through the haze the dog awakens me. It stands and breathes and makes me
look. Embroidered night. Pelt-skin and pushing nose.
Is it come this time. Gaze looking hard at something which is me. Comes into here
these nights handing me nothing but
this gaze—*you, you*—and again now it
insists—looks hard then looks
away. Leery but intimate. Thinks like a
shovel, digs. Spotted torso. Never forgets anything. Says this is how the
burning of being feels—*nothing*—something of moths beating trapped wings in the
air—air spotted too—air saying *I am still here* or *it* is or *she*
is—dog
nudges hard, refusing delay—has no whim—knows not
the *is-it-worth-it* thought, nor decision, nor indecision,
has no self in mirror, sleeps through din then without lifting heavy head watches us
lose reason, lose by reason. Then sleeps again. Hears reasoning resume. Like clotting of
blood. What do we need? Would you bring me some *now* I think, it is more *now* we need—
then there will just be all the
rest—but this version, this which is the only
version, this is where pretending (even if you're not pretending) ends. Just like
that. No extra time to make up later. No later. It's watching me now. It knows how to do the
only thing
as if it were the only right thing. I put my hand on my face. Feel my face. Feel
vertigo, the shut drawer of pennies, everything helping itself to
itself—ash and furies and freckled
splotches of oncoming
dawn. Are you ready? You can only consent now. Anything postponed? Anything you planned
to say, do, think, breed, recall, ask forgiveness for—what

happens to the room *afterwards*? The angle of the light

matters now but in a few hours to whom will it

matter so? And the hornet nest we doused but which still hums holding dawn wind?

I get up again to follow him. Up through one more night's calamity—no, how can it be

                              if you still

breathe in it—feel nighttime sizzle with your breath now rough now soft pouring out

into it—feel breath rippling round your hunched-up self, your almost completely broken

self, feel night to be the mechanism entirely built to proffer the inhale,

recover the exhale—listen—night grabs my

breaths too—pushes this inhale in as if to make it

sleek and tight as it flows through my only

citadel. I'm going to whip right through you it up-

wells, am going to ram forth into all your openings this fine electro-

magnetism, want to ship up, snap up, gut in, gutter through

every bit of you with minutes more minutes. Afterwards

                         this air

                         shall hold no more minutes of

yours, will be all flow, cluster, possibility, speed—stirred but

not stirred-for—no recurrence then—substanceless—oh—keep it

                         substanced—for now

stay in it. Remain clock. Do not spurn earth. Have mass. Electron, spin. Amaze

air. See day. Look it is coming, wait. Wait for the change. Oh the

change. Spur of leaves shaking wind. Dawn wind. Wind of differential. Mother.

                         Be apparent. Be appareled with

self still. What does it know this creature. Because it

knows. I look at its eyes but it does not look at me. It never

does. I look in there. *Tell me.*

Now down the hallway and open the door. You there

in dawnlight in sheets. Are those still sheets. I squint. I make no

breath—hear wind whirl-up the valley out there over trees. Soft

windowpane. Is it now. Hand on the knob I watch the

                         surface of the sheet

as one listens to the seashell for far distances, waiting for the long lament, some blush of air, an ancient boundless

                                    seeking seeking

                                    deliverance—but

the small mound moves, and the humble rise and fall beauties itself

up, and it is like light suddenly speckling shadows and motions on a brick wall

which had been till then reduced to grid, everywhere grid,

and you have not died. Strange and familiar your stillness.

Maybe you are dreaming? Sunrise is

touching the stillness which was night's trees. A light wind

rises. The window pales and fills with things.

I am afraid. I look at the pods' castanets, the sky full of red

shot. Again the dog goes over to your side and settles close. He knows.

Like wheat collapsing onto the threshing floor he sees

how much is left in the gripped hand to spill. A creature that knows joy knows

death. They bind each day in chains at the end. Daylight shows it.

It pierces us with its red spear. It widens.

Oh you out there—run, it is day, run everywhere—

rise fall sink breathe—open up—happen.

WITH MOTHER IN THE KITCHEN

Let us pause. If you could be saved then yes, ok. If you could be contained in life then
yes.
But diligent, foolish, I count off the dates—your days, your breaths—
as if this mistrust of the natural were not enough—
looking for the starting point—
one of these will be your last word—
what will we have just said when you stop—
what will the phrase be which is interrupted by your final breath—
did they warn us about this freedom—
that there are no regulations—
that we do not run out of patience, we run out of time—
they wrench out the life, just like that—
everything is innard and then it is not—
that one day you are no longer at home here—
also that there is no room left, your room runs out—
the next move is no move—
who told us to feel we could settle in—
today they will ask me for your home address, I have one to give—
my beloved unknown, you pour out—
where you arrive is *too far*—
is not an entrance, not an exit—
you have to stop being—
I don't know if it's formless—
no there is no longing—
a bird chirps firmly from the porch—
the genes chirp firmly in the blood, it still flows—
there is still body heat, honor the body heat—

you ask for the meds, honor the meds—

you have gone too far, you cannot turn around,

the flame of the candle blooms, exceedingly if I stare, I stare,

be glad, inauguration of, say little, save breath,

I will press your hand now and there it is—life—it comes in waves,

it will disappear, it has not disappeared,

accept destruction, *accept,* the word quivers …

You passed inspection, can I tell you that.

You were fully searched. Every option. Every cavity.

At every checkpoint, you were. You were not saved.

This is the final one on this side.

I watch your hands. One is lifting a spoon, one is holding onto the folded cloth.

An iridescence—a crazed green—out the kitchen window, spreading *forever.*

A puddle just there at the foot of the tree from last night's rain.

Now sun. Crusty light, gravelly with pocking shadow, excited by wind. New leaves.

First wind today for these new leaves.

Is it this week. We drink our tea.

The knives and forks glitter in their dark drawer.

They will be there after. Hands will lift them as if nothing.

May I cut your meat, may I stir your soup?

"Sometimes walking late at night/I" and

"let us pause on the latter idea for a minute."

First wind new leaves—no, new wind first leaves.

They came out day before yesterday.

Those intervening days, unbroken stillness settled.

Look, it's May I said. They grow. No wastage of energy. Love. Molecules.

Now they flip up, fly back. One is ripped off and slaps against the window pane.

Still citrine-green-new—it sticks fast to the glass.

For a while. We see it.

Do you want to hang out a bit now, here? Do you want to talk about it,

shall we continue?

It just happens this way, you bend to the cup,

the sea-reaching stream runs down

somewhere below our angle of view—

though on a good day you hear it, I see you

hear it—straightening itself as it goes, going down to go faster,

at some point merging and merging, splitting its waters, gathering, a slope will help it.

I'd take my bucket, may I have a sip of you, river, I am so parched.

We wait for it to come, the time.

We are so glad for this wind, it delivers.

The mind too, whirling, vectoring, reaching short but at least

reaching, rising, consigning—towards and towards. Terrible. You've got to

love it, dark mess of words and winter-

unwinding—blaze, gleam, build, tear down. I put the kettle back on. We are on

pause. The change of scale in our thinking has occurred. Planetary death so

what is yours. How big. Where do I put it. You were born. You were in time, were

ahead of time all this time and now we are waiting

for it to go on without you in it. That.

When time will go on and you

will not be in time.

What is it we were just

talking about. Your years. There were mornings dew moon highways nation-states

shame law. I was born. That was just yesterday. *Far far away* you said opening up

the book. I am three. I look at the page. Your hand knows how to turn it so the next thing

comes about. All will be buried in dirt.

DEMENTIA

Where am I now. And *now*? Once there was no other shore.

Now I peer into the other shore.

One day in my life the halo of *event* appeared, re-

placed event. Dolled up and un-

darkening. Something too open opening further. Swept clean. Night round

a lamp, street empty, street gone, the white of this thought whitening

further, a wave sweeps it away, the clenched fist of the present instant—right

here—this one—tightens (I am here) then loosens (where am I). Where? The

clutching of this thought,

cinching further—am I in life-movement, forward—am I the lack of

question, something that can be remembered from much

later on, from afterwards, from tomorrow, is it slow suicide this having thinned

to what will come to be seen as an introduction—were we the first introduction

to what might have been a species—a first try a failure but full of nervous sparks—

we called them vision or

thought—

technopoesis—accelerate, drift, drift—

undetermined, intermediated—all aftermath—spectacular creativity (though just

first draft)(who knows what is to come)(what came)(what could have come)—(if)—,

surveyors, tuners, someone who knocked at a window and wanted to come in, so

violent, these fingers→what they have done and made→so nervous→clawing and
caressing→nothing was left to us but touch→no stories but those of touch→in the right
hand in the left→then torn apart→in→between→just to see *in*→to hear it
squeal→a ringtone? a devil?→always returning to try one more time→to hear it
one more time→the sound of the ripping apart→the inhale of the seeing-in→
perfectly→is *that* perfectly→do you think we really saw it *as it is* this time→pulling

aside the heavy baldachin→brocades from the East, tassels from the South→no Gabriel anywhere in sight→no choir→devices that broke down the human skin, the human mind, now there is

another mind, prefigured by drones→algorithms→image vectors→distributive consciousness→humanoid robotics→what is required now→ is→a demarcation→what is *artificial*→technological end-times now only just beginning→along the watchtowers→pleasures of nihilism, speechlessness, incredulity→not knowing what to do with these hands, these→how they want to inflict pain on the powerless the weak the poor→then the passionate complicit mass-resignation→mass→look there they are in the ditch the means of production→your hands have been cut off and cast down in the midst→soon they will hand your stumps a shovel→you must cover it with dirt the century→action its dialect→and if you bury it→you come to the end of action→the hands will move for a while as they are wont to do→down there in the earth→the thousands cut off each day→millions→then they are still→not even the animals go to them→miles of ditches, countries of hands→ all the action in them stilled→markets stilled→excess fetish vertigo stilled→

So now go back. Touch yourself. Take yourself to yourself. In anger in need. Remember your self. Put the hand in, and from the bottom of the sack cast out the seed, the pesticide, the pests—twist the cap of the pipe—let water flow—combine ingredients—try for that first time the plasticizer—how loathe—a butterfly just emptied itself into untraveled air but you couldn't look up—a butterfly so rare but you can't look up—the reaction has to work—the retardant the photochemical the imitation transformation where the molecules—(now you remember them from school, the first time you knew of them, you *drew* them, the world, its secrets)—must make you lubricant, stronger than anything in the known—and everything non-essential dies—curling, subtracting, coating, re-combining—your plastic-laden ocean bearing grief inside it too. Once—

Once is a place I visited. A flame burns it up. Just looking at it burns it. Once. A lot of coming and going—flame where legs run thundering along the cave the wall where many of us run at once, hooves in the way of escape, and those are not drones that chase from above, that will run us off this high shelf because we cannot stop— *once* has a taste *over the precipice* is the taste *it's all becoming darker* is

the taste—*this minute is pecking at your shell*—that's the sound—percussion is
our mind—this torrent of us pouring into day the paradise the day. I know a day.

Now where am I—and

now? Running and raining I am. Carrying my face before me.
Here where my mind drops down to the stubble of grass—where?—revelation
blinding as a fat stone in sun, my body desperate for concealment—think of

something

else, do you not feel it, this total expression hides you further,
lays itself down over the scribbling of me, the
dream of me, of having me, me stilled and dragged, opened, shared, meat—till all
this bright mind makes what you wanted so to feel—or see—or just *take in*—dis-
appear. I lie by the stream. Grow *accustomed*. Have hooves ears rich flesh hide.
Am hunted. But you knew that. Hunted by the once. Hunted by then. By when. By
when the time comes. By time comes. Time. There you are scribbling me again on
the walls of the cave, my sideways-leaping to avoid you when you pass me,
come around the other side of me, to cut me off from mine, such a small decision and I
am suddenly yours, hide hooves ears flesh, such a small hesitation—where am I now—

in this

representation—as you stroke me onto the wall in flames, unreal, unreal, *you can't
have that* I want to say, that is me, that is what I am, this given, just this, running and
free—you will make towers bridges tunnels hangars wonders, you will have
stone marble cement bustle haggle in doorways—doorways!—chronometers,
managers, mercury in thermometers, saints and virgins—I don't remember where
we are again—we became more—now I am in a cubicle, a tabernacle, a festival,

again say the

leaves in quick wind over my face even though I am trying to go still, grow in-

invisible, take

instruction, excuse this diction, especially here by this fallen tree, scraggly, hung
with webs bees peripheries entropies love

III

TO TELL OF BODIES CHANGED TO DIFFERENT FORMS

In the market of ideas, of meat—in the teeth of need—you will never be happy with
your body—it is not the right body—the shame of having to appear
in it—as if always a few steps behind it—or like a man standing
at the edge of a small river which muscles-by unaware—slipping by—under
reflection—too fast for its own good—making you a fault in perception—a catastrophe to
which a body is joined—disjoined—all headgear, undergear, tied, trussed, confused—
wearing your arms and legs as if waiting for security to find you—shaven then unshaven—
a bit traditional though all at once too raw too sexed-up—shivering portal and obstruction—
seeing yourself there, features amplified, distorted by normalcy—what you are dying to be
eluding you again, a hole in time, in the consolations of light—
sublime heavy weapon of appearance being detonated right there where your eye
meets your eye. I see you. How your apparition shrinks from itself.
It *knows* there was another body it was intended for, another century another love
another consolation—another sentence in which to place the heavy "I"—another
sex race core time—a different artifice—a different flow of faults. What are you dying
                                                        to be. How un-
knowable do you feel, heavy ordnance with no *where* to hit. The thing about history is
it drains it flows but has no borders. Is not this soft smartly turned-out
green grove of summer—no places in it for insemination, iridescence, work—
this being not yet you imitating it, the tiny nationstate which is
you, *your* you. You can't understand it. You can look up at the sublime with its
massive firm edges—albeit under erosion—who cares—you won't be around to see it—
the altered thing—you who so need to *be altered*
that this could be acceptably a *you*—this thing which cuts loose from an other's regard—the
right ghost to be—yes that—a *want* wanting to be all folds all energy—
an image filling itself in as almost but not entirely *matter*. It's late summer.
We will never be happy with the body. Will exchange it for another. Will

change its months name legs arms voice—will shave self off—will watch breasts grow
as the buttonwood grows. The sublime is so alone. It watches us. Have you failed to
                                                        make your
self? Are you still hidden, are you too exposed—it's hard to tell—
perfect losses both ways—too much body, too little—voice too deep or too
void—voice too full of space like a small nail trying to hold in too large
a weight … Erect or not erect enough. Oh are you built yet as you would be
built? Caution: you will make yourself anew. Caution: you will not like the new
one either. After a while you will need to do it again. There is no body which will
suffice. It's a theology—your mucous—it's a post industrial cock or a derivative
cunt—are you getting ahead? Careful: you will get ahead of your self. Indeed, you are
ahead of yourself. I love you for that, says your best friend. I love you for your
                                                        unquenchable dis-
satisfaction—after months so dry, rain came—so quiet at first we did not know what
to make of it. It tapped each thing as if a blind creature coming to see. We
were where it was meant to arrive. Weren't we? It went by too fast. Hard and fast. A kind
of porn. I saw you feel your new ass. You like it but then I saw you wonder whether,
right there where the idea of grandeur taxied down your piste of a brain, ready to go
but on queue—who knows how long it will be before you take off—and by then, wouldn't it
                                                        be old hat …
Warning: by then a new idea will have popped up. As if the runway weren't long
enough or the sky too small. Change! The debt ceiling has shown itself to us. The un-
doing has shown its cheek, the lovely small of its back, the laminate skin of its sex
appeal—there may be nothing else behind these words—by definition—caution—they too
seek to be changed, they feel unseen, unheard, mis-shaped, mis-
understood. Caution: you can be neither filled nor consumed. Caution: you are not
beautiful—there is no such thing—you are a forced withdrawal from an occupied
terrain—that's what a body is—once you are out you want to go back in—not to the
same place exactly—but back in, back in—the same defiling of your corpse so that you
                                                        can be re-
surrected as a new you-and-me thing. Look a small mudwasp is building a nest.
Its activity wrenches the open air. There will be but this one. It will abandon its young

never to return. It is doing a form of research. The mud is powdery like the foundation I have applied, looking so complete to myself in this mirror in this instant before the

light changes and

I must begin again.

SELF PORTRAIT: MAY I TOUCH YOU

here. May I touch your

name. Your

capital. May I

touch outcome, kindness, slur down my caresses to

throat, eyes, end of the tunnel. Come out. Now your name is changed. How do I reach

right name, right bandage—the character that you will be for now

in the dark, where there is need—is there still need?—can you be for this short time

singular? You need to be singular. There you are changing again. These words are

furrows. Now they are

arrows. Don't touch where it says no. It says no everywhere. Where is the spot where you

are faking it. That spot. So well. Can you tell. Doesn't work for you. What works for you.

The rouge you have applied to see who you would be for a while. You

change your mind. You change the shade. You recognize yourself for a while

then it grows old. The pupae in the mud grow old. They've slicked it smooth as skin with

perfect perforations. All entrances and exits. The only way, right way, the pupae morph

to their winged

stage and grow. They exit not to return. Those who laid them do not return. They

change from

unborn to being here now, 67 degrees under the eaves as they come out. I watch. Nothing

can change out here in the given. It is given and it is received. If ants find the pupae

they eat the nest through. Sometimes they get to live their life. I know you need to be

a significant player in

the creation of

your veri-

similitude. Abide abide. Do you do nude. Can I touch your apparition, your attitude,

multitude, your eternally misunderstood solitude—do you do adulthood, husbandhood,

motherhood—listen: sap in the dogwood—not like blood, crude, flood, lassitude—I want you

to come unglued—clad in nothing but blood—in it—dripping wet—appearing always re-
reappearing,
of course wearing your camouflage—whatever you currently identify as—clad in your
surface your newest reason—may I touch it—your phantom your place-
holder, undelivered, always in the birth canal, undiscovered—your personal claim on
the future, residue of all the choices you've made thus far, also the purchases, invoices, in
voice where your change resides, in vice where it settles—skin—a win win—the management
wishes to express concern—can I touch there where you appear in the mirror—where you lay
your simulacra down—lave the mercurial glass—bypass being—hardly a *ping* where you
boomerang—here you are back outside—ghost money—

do you not want to feel

the fierce tenacity of
the only body you can sacrifice—the place where it is indeed your
fault—there *in* the fault—no heartsearching? Me with my hands on the looking glass
where your life for the taking has risen, where you can shatter into your million pieces—
all appareled refusal. What are you a sample of today—
what people.

INCARNATION

What shape am I? A vote? An invoice? How much do I
count. Am I a verity. Run your hands over me. There.
What is a lie—hurry—make meaning—liquidate tense—
outwit the wind—no, outwit intimacy—harvest it—fake a
common dream—say *touch me* to the failing grip—of time—
it fails—the sound of decay also exists on skin—your skin—
are you all covered—is the residue wiped off, is debt, waste,
love—feel it, this *awareness of* your shape—what's left after
the comments-section shuts—see what that makes of you—
or is it me—when will the fade begin, why this eternal close-
up, this wiry sinew of gaze threading into each pore, the
meeting place—where you are most speechless—most—
there is no word for it—don't know any—say house—say
don't go one step further—say don't turn around you are all

front—smell it the scent of time, it is skin, is all this forward-
facing you cannot back out of—I'm going into my name—I'm
touching my cheekbone—draw me my outline—make the
skull very loud—the chalk on the sidewalk quivers
slightly—once I had a father—I touch my face it is wet—
there was a year I forgot to look—I was a child—my shape
seemed a brushstroke—a thing about to be said out of
respect for something or someone who had to arrive soon
because we had built a system based on waiting and every
thing—love respect fear—was based on waiting—
so then you would be given your shape—and so be
honored—there was a racket but that was childhood—
everyone was screaming all the time but that was words—
the past tense was like a bolt of cloth you could touch and

lift and it would float in the air for the briefest time as if it
were time—or the curtain—teaching you to see shape—
wind in its muslin—filled with light, with turns, then sucked
back in—flat against the wall. Then dropped. Like that.
Nothing more. Can a gazelle hold as still. Oh accelerationism.
The *thing* in you now able to be *not seen*. And so there you
are. In the lull you can *not be*. Or not be *seen*. They began by
merging. A thing penetrated you, then it withdrew. You are
something's thing and it grabs your shape. It yanks your
hair. Pulls back your face. You take its shape in you. A forced
occupation. A patient ministering force inside. *We must be in
common.* This is our little market. Dark, dark, we are making
our own futures-market, organizing seed, oozy excess, in
thrall, unstoppable, breaking into the sealed-up skin-thing,

minutest interview, burning with love, detained, breath
obtaining, yes abstract but not so much there is no
torture. See. It is small and private although you can still
scream. The crucial parts even here redacted. As we come
together. Like this thing you are holding. Life inked out of it.
Its true shape escaping you. That is how meaning works.
Holding this place in place. Cosmic nihil. Chemsex. Extended
peak. Death in hyperdrive—that shape of yours—we have to
blur it—sand it—pixilate it—rush, froth, dismember. Even a
stickfigure is too much. Even a cartoon in which you bend
and rise, bend and rise, to give invention its pleasure, is not
full enough of all the seed-in-wind body wants. Oh little
revolution. You must come to an end in stasis of course.
It is not pleasure but you will think it is. In these notes from

apocalypse feel the shape of becoming machinic. How it
holds you in place. Go ahead raise your hand to your mouth.
Taste it, the stagnation. Bring it upon yourself. Accelerate.
Immediate. Be incessant. Be disindividuated. When you

were born from me I heard in your cry the loneliness. A wish
came out. Was the first thing. All my decisions have been
wrong. That face of yours just come from me I will never see
again. Everything subsequent was flame that could speak.
Wanting and empty. Full of purchasing power. Glass shatters
in my mouth as I try to say this. *Here* said the light as you
entered it. Here is *more*. Gauzy light surrounded you and
you were gone, you were in, you were unwrapped from non-
being, it was the last I saw of you, I saw a line of elms out the
window and they went on, you were raised up, white wrap

of belonging, instant addiction to breath, I watched it start
you up, *too late too late* I was thinking in the laughing light,
make her whole again, put her back in the unshaped, make
her nobody's business again, invisible girl how I would have
cast the light off you, pushed your hollow chest back up,
head first, got you out of the mediation. But a tube was put
in. You *lived*. The body you were sunk-into washed up on
this shore. With its urgent message no one would ever hear
of course. As if you were the waste product of some
unstoppable subtraction, some buzz the stars thrilled in
messaging their absence, their methods of absence, their non-
irruption from shapelessness—the place without war. And
the nurse's chemise she covered up, to keep the stain off.
I wanted you to stay inside, my life, you, coming out of un-

shape, you permanent now, dying and permanent. What
shape does lie take which is not the *right* shape. All shapes
of lie are its right shape. The star's edge, the orchid's rushed
rim, self-empowerment, the breeze just now—the day I am
in—the shape of the trap before it snaps shut, the calm
keyhole holding its key not quite tight, that it lock us in, that

it let us out—what shall we be let out *of*—into what shape—
I don't fit—don't fit what I think—sturdy little wheeling,
going always forward, glaring, whose picture am I, terminal,
not quite terminal, over-expressing cells, overwhelmed with
self improvement—then something goes wrong—this will
not fit—I do not fit—in place—am forgetting my shape
again—must remember it—have to be a clean fit—good
fit—true fit—a truth—no—how can I be that—they kill you

if you don't dream—make sure to dream—that's the point—
it's a shape that won't fit in you, that's why it floats and tears
and wakes you in terror—it is your dream—dream it—
whimper a little ok but touch yourself—feel that hip bone,
the soft of that belly, move slowly, your counterpart is
somewhere you will never find—the one place it is *not* is in
that horror the mirror—that delirium put before you—look
how it waves—you stare again—*what shape am I*—I have to
get it right, is it possible we are alive to get this one thing
right—you peer in, is it a collection of notes just beyond
hearing—what were you to *make*—*that* shape—and how
you would love to sit down again about now, right here in
front of the house, where the dogwood is making its million
shapes—oh dogwood *your* stars are not dead—you would

like to sit and have no one see you—get rid of the baggage,
the footprints—the small blue god that accompanies you
everywhere, saying make sure to be you, be true to your
outcome, your only shape depends on it—am right here it
says, don't think about truth, would be a mistake, think
about nothing but where you end where it begins—*what is
the it* I say—I plead I wait a second to see if it will answer for
once, the small useless god—it sounds like 2000 miles of

shorebreak at once, but small and only around me, given me
that I *be here*, the one thing that betrays me every day, what
you imagine you see me by, the thing all round me so full of
future, like a lining, furry with minutes as I walk through the
waiting, the *waiting for the end*—so much *forever* to be in till
the forever stops—a line all round me you take to be me,

you take it, you take me, the me you take is I agree a
possibility, but it is just one, a surmising, a guess—but you
touch—you reach out, touch, say it—you say the one word
which attaches to me, which has from my first breath—my
name—put down there, certified—proof of live birth—it is
so persuasive—really I have to go, I have to go now—I can't
stand how it tries to hold me, get your stickiness off of me,
you are something they put on a piece of paper, a
momentary idea they had in mind, they put it by my only
time, my arrival time, I am awash in it, they hooked me up in
it, rinsed me clean of me and shaped me firm in it—look
they signed for me—they dated the purchase—it was a good
price—the perfect price, the shape of my price—the making
sense of the shapeless thing I was—which was pushed down

through egg and cell and faith and today's shopping spree—
and all this waiting—and limitation braiding clarification
thinning me out, stretching me out—there was an old friend
I would have liked to have stayed with but I was taken, I was
cleansed of shapelessness and plasmaed and celled-
up and moleculed to death till I started to sprout and divide
again—pushing pushing pushing are these minutes—I feel
myself in the dark as I must have the very first time, when
these fingers formed, just enough, who is this, why is it here,
why can I touch it—and I move across and there is bone and
silk vagueness forms on it—I would brush it off but it is now

part of me, no, not part, it is whole, it is becoming one thing,
all the parts are coming together—a perfect market—
everything in its aisles before the doors open, the opening

bell upon us, any minute now, the chute will open, I will be
received, I will finally be what I am being assembled for, the
parts all slid in till you can no longer tell them apart, there
are no parts, there is a whole, here you go, you have to be
this skin-tight thing and then something celestial barely
skips a beat and that beat is you, you are the next note, they
want you to think it's a song, a great aria—someone hacked
in to the non-existent and introduced this mutation and the
mutation can only grow, now the limbs have formed, they
can touch each other—and there are two of you it
seems—but you must hold them together and say I am one, I
am, here I come now—pigswill, mix, motion, eddying, curl—
original expression, bellied, bald—yards and yards of cells
strung so tightly in, starting to express, disturbing

endlessness, disturbing unceasing: here. Come in to end. I
snip you off. Come in. Who are you. Begin the ceasing now.
A big inhale. Fill you up nice. And then the other part.
Which exhales, lets you go. Easy exit. Running your hand
through what's left of your hair. In yr privates. On yr head
where it flames. Forgive me you say to the creature in the
mirror—I wanted to make you happy. I slip my glasses off to
try to see. I really mean it. I don't know how to transmit
meaning to you in there, mercurial. A redbird flits through.
Look it is gone to both of us now. I would have had you keep
it. I would have had it be in *your* hand, had it still you, had it
make you have—as it has—arrival, shape, meaning—a say
in things. A say in things. In things. A thing.

FROM INSIDE THE MRI

                                                            —my sub-
tropical dancer, partner, or is it birdchatter I'm hearing now, vein in,
contrast-drip begun, everything being sung in the magnetic field's no-upward-rung
unswerving tiny dwelling—you earthling—awaiting your biochip—
they are taking tranches of the body which is one—which has been one all of my life—
can you hear me, he says, squeeze this if problems arise he says, ok? ready? *if if if if*
if yes if yes—here's this to worship—*hi hi hi hi—hi hi high high—*
high high not not not not highnot highnot not not—are you
                                                            ok—next lasts
three minutes—ready? yes?—*not not not not be be be be notnot bebe notnot bebe*
                                                            next one one
                                                            minute—*yes—yes yes yes yes*
yes yes yes yes—can you hear me—next one will last

forever. Question: were you looking up at the cherry all these long weeks. All during
the bombing the destruction of land home flesh the taking of refineries
the turning point the dam which if they breach it will eliminate the
town the graven images the mosques the waterworks the UN School—the idea of
                                                            shelter—Question: the children
                                                            here—in lock-
                                                            down—
Question: "during"?—Question: their being in solitary no food no light no mattress no
                                                            latrine months
                                                            go by only who knows what
                                                            days are, the mind

                                                                you make

                                                        for

dream is taken from them—*during all that time*—Question: this will last a
while—the guards cracking spleen for no reason—four down on one child—his head
cracked against the wall "for sleeping in class"—"I saw blood and feces
on the floor"—"I look away" the teacher says "or they will come

                                                        after me

                                                        next." *All this*

time where are→*are* you→the sap moving and the other fluids moving→the
                                                        crystalline
chemistry of necessity driving the pressure up→into the xylem tubes→
                                                        the tree just
there→outside window→and I want to say yes→yes I hear it→the water
evaporating from each leaf→how it tugs on water remaining in the xylem→
from roots to shoots→sostenuto now staccato→in the violin→in my earbuds→
the children on Sinjar made to flee during this dying→of thirst→during this
trying→to escape→the water molecules stretch the bonds→breathe in→you can
make empty space more empty→yes→you can take from there and make
this fruit→*emptiness*→yes→you can hold it in your eye→its pupil hard→its
                                                        size your
instrument→Question→think of the silence during May's growth you did not hear
buried in this August day→Question→you glanced again at the blossoms and then you
suddenly forgot again→think *during this*→think *time passed*→the more you stretch it
                                                        the more it pulls
                                                        back→
no one knows exactly what does the pulling→it is not gravity→no→another
force→negative pressure brings it up→though all this could exist in
                                                        empty space→vacuum is
full→of energy→and other intangibles→listen→liquids *stretch*→listen→and if you

pull on them ("under certain conditions") they pull back→have
tensile strength→can resist being turned to vapor→worst fears remain for Yazidis
still trapped on the mountain→on the run AP repeats→at this minute→
live in this time zone→look it is a terror it is a hero a heron→it is
                                                    the screen
where history ripens→the mountain so barren→the scream of
the refugee→running towards the chopper→listen→hear this→they
drop bundles of water→the waterman a god under the chopper which hovers, which
                                                    will not
land→so that the boys are climbing now→onto its mechanism→it is a
                                        schism→another one→the gun
just over the hills→the rifleman on his Humvee→the ombudsman, tribesman
fisherman, herdsman, your patron→sharpen your question→is there
more "him" of him with the gun pointing at you→the just-dug pit
fills up like a comment box→I told you not to come→suddenly

seeing the buds that all along, unknown, unbeknownst, unmapped, un-
owned, unnamed, greened—a tableau vivant—oh celebrated
labyrinth, friend—beware pride—keep looking—keep looking
closer—there is a dryness coming but not only of the heart—it
stays outside—helpless as a sea to stop its rigor—as if a last
prize for us—a warm kiss gone too far—but the buds
turn in my breast my dark seat—know nothing of the soldier, of deep time, self harm—
wait and see says the sun rising over all of this at every instant—
365→24/7→wait and see, and→*hi hi hi hi hi hi hi hi*→
almost done he says, you ok—*if if if if yes if yes if*→
and if you think it could be a bird it could be→although it could be the ringtone of the
smartphone someone in the adjacent booth to mine left on in locker 5→which was
not silenced→which can from here be→just made out→
beyond the slurring whooshing impenetrable door→above which

one red light is

singing-out

chamber in use. And the bird sings. On its short loop, its

leash, it sings, here it is, here it comes again. *Chi chi trillip trillip*

chiuuu chip chip. No

matter

what you do, you are free. It is a nightmare. You are entirely free. There now,

careful now. You can go.

PRYING

(For Dr Barbara Smith)

As if I never wake from this blackout again, again this minute they lay it out
on the wheeling transporter, so silent, then the surgical table,
my body, my citizen, anesthesiologists back from coffee break, cables
on mylar headrest taking my head down now, arms into armlock,
then positioners, restraints—day talk
all round—the guidewires in, the intravenous ports, the drip begun.
An/aesthesia by which is meant the sensation of having sensation blocked,
a collapse of response, *a total lack of awareness of loss of*

> *awareness—*

on the wall, snapshots of the chosen few training on

> the new

> robotic patient-

> lookalikes—my only

body—memories, contritions, facts—
oaths, broken oaths, my piece of path into the
labyrinth—how far have I reached in—and in my flesh these
rapid over-rhyming cells, which want us to go faster, faster, headlong with
mirth ruth glee—what would they *be*—searching for
what minotaur, yarn in hand spooling-out mad towards core, eager for
core—all's underneath—readout's small *ping*s beginning on the screen. They will
learn everything about me while I sleep. I sleep the sleep of those wanting to live.
I sleep the sleep of those wanting to be left alone by life. And
safe. With guarantees. Here take the keys. I should wake up. It's hard
accepting to *be free*. It is not true. You must be still and not resist. Are you
completely readable now. To survive, you need to be

> completely

> readable. So I

accede, I sign the dotted line, they will keep track
of everything, my breaths, my counts, my votes—invoices, searches, fingertips—don't I
                              know you
from somewhere says my heart to the machine reading me out, didn't I give you my
                              code, my pin, my blanket
                         permission
to suppress the last revolution, to calculate the timing of
                              the solstice the pressure
                              cooker depth of
                              ice core and whom
                              do I have
                              locked away
down there—do you not see them—don't look away, the
dials are set—where is the nearest job—no gauge picks up their screams at the
employment line, the checkout where the food is not enough, it is so
quiet here, who am I signing on to be,
and then—oh—here it comes again, here in this moment I shall recall
however long the life is after this
when you look down at me and stare and your long arm offers its hand, cold hand,
and I offer you mine—we hold—then we repair,
you in your disposable surgical blue hair-cap, blue mask, I in mine,
down, down through this operating theater's novocaine-green
gleam, its cellophane membrane, serene, clandestine borderline &
your life depends on what says the disappearing air, the dis-
appearing vein, surveil me here, in solitary, entertain me mise-en-scène,
hear me chain of command, touch me, stain-free middle class American
female subject starting downtown on the drip line,
on the gleaming staff of this protean sentinel, its silver rod
held up, torchful of forgetfulness, streaming, translucent, give me your
mass, your teeming cell-dividing
mass—give me your poverty,
your every breath is screened, your every cell, it is not hit and
miss, we get it all, your safety lies with us, hold still,

granted it's cold at first, this new relief, your icy nation thanks you

for the chance to test these absolutes on you

murmurs the gleaming staff in the deliberate air, astir,

toe-separators being pulled on now and leggings next,

always a bit tighter that the blood flow fast in this undercover

slow maneuver, whirr, blink, you get a little extra life as a reward—for what I

cannot see—what these concentrates of vigilance push into me,

capital and knowhow and all these minutes, minute—where to

finish off the string and bite the knot, erotic dead-end, no jobs,

the virtualization, the play of nerves, no jobs, they jab

the last bit quick—paradise confusion sedative—oh and the re-

bates the debates and the womb what was that really,

the total concentration of capital, the ten commandments, Job that

heartthrob now standing right before me here as the drip-line on its silver rod,

its one arm up, its other out into this widening avenue

                               to step you off this

                               luminescent curb

                               to hail what cab

the ghosts in their scrubs do not perturb, bitstreamed, stubbing the blood

where the small mound of flesh is grabbed, flap scabbed, snip drip as it is all

transcribed by the robotic arm, prosthetic mind, rich text, as she unslacks her

matchless stitch, having detached, having reattached, no speech in

them, bleached light, fleshtrim, mutation, division, over-expressed, under-

                               suppressed—held still

by your long hand, transnational, undersea cable, invisible ministration,

and when you take mine into yours

                               you say under-

                               stand,

                               we are taking the first steps friend

towards the longest journey, community,

breakers of codes, corporate raiders, west of everything, no immunity,

put on your hat your wrap be ready now to take my hand its certainty its

                               purity—

there will be no one come to fetch you back from here—
you must now take this voyage out yourself alone
to reach the peerless place hard to think-in, squint-in,
you will not be embarrassed there is nothing to reveal,
you are a shoo-in as the heroine, new citizen, back since the pleistocene,
being touched up like a virgin engine in the squeaky clean saline
punchline, your soul at plumb-line, magic marker written in in print
to make sure LEFT *is* left, it's not benign this timeworn
zone in you, no not benign this fast archive,
surgical thread making its dragline in the artificial
moonshine—how supine must the whole apparatus of *being* get,
shop-talk above you now a serpentine acetylene,
you under here endlessly re-learning the only story—abasement, abasement—
and here is my hand it says, slide yours into it, come now, radiant,
                                                    astringent,
this river's here for you to enter now, obedient, in payment,
you in it now as it comes into you, your profit margin, look—
flowers falling without attachment—
weeds growing without detachment—
slide under now into ignorance—
there is no evidence, also no continuance—don't mispronounce
your lifesaver, also a bit of fever, it too a visitor, and no I
cannot augur, also there is, in truth, no aftermath, just this new kind of
stalker—your personal flyover—your tiny temporary stopover,
and obviously no ecstasy in your surrender you have no choice also no
underwriter, take my offer—and I
did—and when I went home later I had a cup of tea
and made a call to her cellphone to get the unfortunate results
but we are not there yet, still have the void here to traverse
across this page which is a wide expanse and will these very words if perfectly
                                overheard
                                see me through
                                was the question

as the cold came on,

me hoping to do nothing wrong then hoping for a bargain,

asking how long before one would be able to live again *as if—*

and those other turns in the brine—the *yet—if not,*

if now, and now, when now—turn towards me now a bit you say to them and then

let's turn the torso this way please recheck marked spot.

Can see the guidewires but can no longer feel them.

Then the thing on the other side, the person who will open up my hand and say

it's over now can you hear me here is some water.

And in my room cut flowers still in their paper stapled up. Undelivered.

And you get a little extra life to live now—here—can you still live it.

CRYO

Now they say you are ready for a long stilling voyage. Is it further into nature. A life of make believe. I have no idea what is retained. What is here is certainly not there. The bad news became apparent too late. The day became all one day and was done. We got rid of the calendar, the book of side effects, the weather, the fairy tales. We would like the monster back. We want the fight with the monster, his bright sure nothingness, back. He walked towards us firmly once. We were equipped with our long sharp object. The *what happens*. We were provocative that is for sure. But we tried to listen. To nature. It suggested we forego proof. It suggested we try mimicry. Empathy. The filigree of syntax wailed. It coursed out our throats as if we weren't even there, gentle then ungentle, burned-out on persuasion, for centuries.

But hi. I've been having an interesting discussion with→those who pass their lives on→hastily assembled→dimly aware of the reasons for their wanting to become inanimate→an entity no longer human→an interloper→a possible manifestation, an impersonal person, an impersonation→an apathy from both emotive and organic color→a form of leap→from looper rover lopen→to run away→proto empathy→no memory→no entity. A leap from one sort of being, one sort of being immaterial to another. A possible alien subjectivity. Not idle but at the furthest reaches. Of empire. No song. Downward. Toward the stone terrace. You do not suffer you do not lie in waiting. Without a subject. The self a mere occasion for the swarming of responses, oh weariness, we can suspend, responses can suspend, letting certainty reach apogee, yes, would glance at me furtively but then I, I

hi→I narrate continuity→not what is wanted except absolutely→what is said in my absence→is→my absence→they complimented→me→consistencies orders summaries outcomes→no berries on *that* bush→arranged terror→I see saints gathering→see enlarging grasps of order→understand this as likeness→is not→ visit the clinic→experience swarm fragment→during his increasingly rare visits he→we are left in the uncertain state→196 below centigrade→has not yet experienced information death→can only begin after legal death→when?→motion to lose→grief suction cold→precise unaffronted damnation→cryopreservation→ preserve my brain information→this peyne was bitter and sharp→this paine driede uppe all the lively spirities of flesh→blodlessed and paine-dried within→ blowing of the winde and colde coming from without→mete togeder in the swete body→jittery→of Crist→of→

now my no-me comes round, my most silent me, too fine, exposed, figuring a stray completeness, not done but casting away all edges, inside there is nothing, however small there is nothing, with its own hue—void, ultimate, but not final—turning back on itself to find no self coming to the edge of the done the said—

I am sorry to want this—but it flows turning so fast through what electromagnetic field saying I'll wake not, I'll with existence not exist, I'll nestle in unattainable reality, anticipating, beyond intellect, awaiting rain, diminished to where I can find nothing to give, nothing to give myself to, everything is, nestling in, unfound, whirling through no transformation, at one sudden point I came to surrendering, sufficiency having split up and used up but not all→nothing coming from anywhere→time wraps.

Glanced furtively around.
Becoming unhitched from the animal.
Tried to frame our response.
Our ending was nothing like—
We are beholden we say.
We are so beholden we think.
The shadow narrative has been scratched away.
A blight, a damp, a leaching sees us coming.
Yes we know we are interlopers.
Where did he go she asks?
The narrator, the thing, or someone else?
No pathology found.
Maybe just an aberrant causal loop.

As in the next sentence.
So we introduce the period.
It is not coming back.
Is in this sense absent while clinging to time.
You might find yourself standing on a bridge
looking upriver. You are clinging to
the top of its milky white stairs.
You need to push. That is artificial light.
Have you known depth to be true?
Here in this period of *ludicrous attachments*.
You cannot close down meaning.
You close down meaning.
There are tinny machine sounds.
How can it matter if it has meaning.

The life of

My illness

Non artificial intelligence

Are these the last words we say. Will we be talking about what we have just
talked about. You put the pen down. It lies there without moving.
The body is stiffened by something happening far away→though the curious bag
inside beats like a heart still→like a line repeated→an opinion from the
future→low, repeating some science→looking back at that prayer that was not
received→and in this was brought to my mind this word that Crist sayed "I
thurst"→for I saw in him a doubille thurst one bodely and another gostly→the body
dried alle alon long time with wringing of the nailes and weight of the body→the
skinne and the fleshe that seemed of the face and of the body→was smalle rumpelde
with tawny coloure→like a drye bord when it is aged→period of ludicrous
cognition→suddenly in the next mode of sentience→who is the "he" that cannot
exist without him→mechanical doll comment section woman of no
reputation→even this ATM requires interpretation→impassable, broken, asked

if she needed "anything beyond the venom"→the "he" of the next paragraph already hanging on to this→blodless and paine dried within→blowing of the winde and colde→coming from without→met togeder in the swete body of Crist→it was a dry harre wind, wonder colde as to my sighte→and paine folowing that he was blodless hanging uppe in the eyer→as men hang a cloth to drye.

IV

DOUBLE HELIX

One bird close up by the house   crow
makes the wall's temporariness
      suddenly exist
      one call into
the arrival of the storm the announcing
by flocks and swarms
      the flowerbeds turning in the solar system
      listen—
Schubert and the thrush at once and
      somewhere in space we
      hang are hanging
      also the red dress on the line I rush to get to
in time
also the slack in the line up-snapping then down
      what scale this pitch-
      changing slapping
of the cotton-poly blend listen and my approaching
arms rising to catch the
      ties my hair blowing over it onto it behind us
      from the open door the violin and beside us
at the edge of the woods the last of the thrush—
      can we hear them
      these flowerheads being carried in this solar system
      sepals receptacles—the vascular bundles
inside the stems—
      near the blown-open door the strings' diminuendos—

also these hatchlings in their nest in the eave in the storm born in it
wrapping round them thunder twigs bits of mylar dusk
also accuracies of the
built porch of day of
the negative forcing, the solar constant, the
storm nonstop though modulating round these
dime-sized heads—in each
the magnetic chip and round it the tiny shellfish-crushable skull—
Venus is almost big as Earth was lush at origin had
oceans imagine yet has no
water anywhere
today. Venus
had runaway
greenhouse. Could Earth. Of course we know it could he says
at the podium which fits in my head in the spot for under-
standing,
the question is rather how long
before runaway
occurs
one bird now
close up by the white house on the green hill (crow)
like a lockpick
one caw one
into the wildly cursive announcing by flocks and swarms
as somewhere in space we turn are
turning,
the final snowball Earth was followed promptly
by the Cambrian explosion
he explains
then eukaryotic cells with membrane-bound nuclei
expanding rapidly into eleven different body plans

which eleven still encompass
>all creatures ever to inhabit Earth—
>at the edge of the woods now the thrush
>being sung out entirely by
>this thrush—
>the whole forest moving—
under the eave the just-hatching new ones in
>thunder
>in their
>having been born
>in it—
>*this is what is*—
what will the sunshine tomorrow feel like
>for the first time striking them
>skulls necks eyeslits
>tightening everything
>creaking, pushing open the immense door—
power down now but us in here scanning the screen
>for the emergency we are in to appear *here it is*
and the sound of the flapping of water
>in wind—
>and the sound of the nations gathering
for their final
>negotiation,
>everyone trying to speak in
>whole sentences, listen,
they keep breaking, the suitcases fall open, the
>inky speeches
>wash away in the downpour, what
>will the delegates say now, listen,
>it is 1965 in Selma, Alabama, the schoolboy is beginning again

his first-ever assignment in his one-room school,

      he shall scratch a word

      onto the blackboard,

whose turn is it he thinks chalk in hand

and will there be someone on the other side of this to meet me

      on the other side of this word if I spell it out correctly

      it is simple and powdery and made of

      seven letters—

the force of the black is impossible to touch—

      he stands there like a breeze still thinking he is dreaming

the dream he is late again for school but he is

      not. He is on

      time. It is his

      turn. Who

is the teacher. What is that he feels at his back in his

      shoulders. He looks at

his hand. Its swirling small shadow

      round the still stick

      of chalk—

from where in the earth

      did it come

      this piece of moonlight, piece of

      dead coral.

Oh good dark he whispers to the black behind the shadows,

      the hand-shadow being cast by his one self on the dark,

      by the single lightbulb behind him the

      hum,

his own knuckles here and the tightly-clenched fingers

wrapped like a bird-beak hard

      round the chalk

gripping something to bring home

      to the nest—

because it must be
       shoved down
       into the newborn, this cursive—must be
       forced in—
that they be made to inhabit
       another day—
       it is so simple—
and the next-on curl—and the billowing handshadow
       over each spot he need mark—
and how nothing can
       stop it
       this our mineral
       imagination
       as here now
       on this page
this uniball pen
       shall write
       if I make it
       his word out completely
       over this
       void

THE MASK NOW

Dying, Dad wanted sunscreen. Nonstop. Frantic if withheld. Would say
screen, and we just did it. Knew he was dying. Was angry.
In last weeks wore red sleepmask over eyes day and night. Would
ride it up onto his forehead for brief intervals, then down, pulled by
hand that still worked. A bit. Sometimes shaking too much so just
cried *eyes*. Cried *now now*. Once cried out *light*—more like a hiss—was
there for that. Yanked it quick. Needed it so badly, the bandage, the

world is a short place, wanted the illustration of it gone, wanted to not
see out, wanted no *out*. But I am guessing. The vineyards down the slope,
each latent bud beginning to plump. In the distance, mountains. Beyond
sea. All of it distraction, but from what. A waste of what. The red
sleepmask. I should have burned it with the rest but kept it. The pane
made trees look painted on. Silky. Not good silky. In the next valley once,
hammering. Thought it human at first. The woodpeckers went on for

days. A carnival of searching for void. How full void is. Small tufts of
grass growing so that I can keep track. *Taking root is not an easy way to
go about finding a place to stay.* Maybe nothing would happen after
all. The hollowing-out now added to by crickets. Spiders making
roads in sky. I watch. Look *at*, then *through*. What is the empty
part? Where. Can find nothing that is empty. Seems I should, and soon, as
where would he go, or what would the indented place on the bed where

he had been *be*. Be *full of*. He was a settler in that flesh, that I could see.
Not far from breaking camp. Wrapping up the organs in their separate
parts—skin rolled away, eyes rolled elsewhere, the fingers tossed
aside—ash, ash—the whole like a dime toss, whom do I love, what part,
what's in the *whom*, what's in the *late*, is there actually a *too late*—

because if there is I do not grasp it. *Mask* he calls, unable to get into
wheelchair any longer, stares for bit of time into the air out front, past

feet, out the glass door, to the olive tree and fig. Is there fire in the
distance. Squints once back up the ray of light, up, back its long road.
How far. *Mask now.* The cremation-decision driving its roots through us
all—roots spreading wildly beyond the shadows of the head. "Neighbors"
will continue to feed stump, book says, long after it is cut, will send it
sugars, phosphorous, nitrogen, all the surrounding trees will try, via
fungi, root hairs, send carbon, send enzymes, whole forest hears

stress signals, will mourn, like the elephant—"I've wrapped stumps in
black plastic when they've refused to die" says Leila, location Wellington,
posted 4 years ago on *permagardening*. But then guard down. Eyes gone.
A red cotton mask. An old TWA one. Elastic gone. Cries out if it slips off.
Wants blue blanket. Says *blue.* Angry. Who was not angry. Nothing
enough. Wants to see all daily tests. Read the bloodwork. Wants trans-
fusions which we withhold. Would open him to infection. Would buy no

time. I'm wearing the sleepmask now. I'm trying it on. Rubberband soft
with age. Adding more age. American red. Red full of noise, of artificial
time. Feels like my face is painted on. A spirit. Upturned, ancient, without
expression. An old stream flows alongside. Glimmering tongues promise
the vanishing will be swift. It's a lie. The periphery disappears but I can
still feel it, our *knowing what's coming* a thicket we got lost in—till the
only thing is *now—mask* my spirit screams—mask now—vacancy

not coming fast enough—first we have to traverse the riddling
disappearances—*extinction* says the mask—go away now I do not want
to see you any longer—beauty you are too near—too near—I hear a
blackbird and the shoo of air where it lifts off—why won't you just
go, you circling winds leaves birds systems directions visibles invisibles
honeysuckle limbs and rose gaining self-song, motion, entering this
continuum—oh continuum do not lie to me with this delicate weight of

time, this floating of *as ifs* and *further-ons* and all your guides to dreaming, abundance, the coming true of the true. No. From under here, listening hard, light feels around me almost visible, doused with benzene, and time goes away, and my eyes feel on them the small weight, the minuscule *no* to things, which I can conjure, which I think I know by heart, but no, I do not, I need the mask. And it feels like an idea. We are in a cave now. It is a hundred million years ago. They will

bring the meds again now and the urine pot—he yells for it—but for now under the mask it is a lowly spot, you can make dawn come, you can feel us *inherit the earth*, the jay shifts in the tree and you can hear it. There is little. You hear the little. Hear the head snapped on the stem. Hear the angel trapped in the stone. Hear pure chance which sounds like a boy marching alongside an army wanting to enlist. The year is 1490, 380, 1774, 10 BCE. You hear the outline in the tree—why—

because it touches the other outlines. If I try to raise the mask the hand he can barely use flutters angry bird wing at me. Would hit me with finger wings but too broken. Maybe in Lee's army, maybe in Grant's. It made no difference in the end. Maybe in Caesar's maybe in Christ's. The trillions seem more clear than ever in the day behind the mask. The dark grey of the fever feels every inch of the bark. Freckled, the pure proclamations being made by the light. It is not day it is saying, bright as

quicklime, text of flames he can hear—no, not day—day sprawls under to let us flow through over its parched back. Lies flat. Lie flat day he thinks under the red mask. Spread yourself over us light, the dead at Antietam yes his people, both sides, the cufflinks in the drawer he will not see again—they were Lee's he would say—they were Grant's—I saw the will of the Davis' side—I did—he says, smell of gravel coming from the path, day sitting now over us like a lioness. It is neither dark nor light. As if you are the place where the branch was sawed off—that place on the oak—and air silently touched your new raw end. You put it on, you pull it down, and then effort, enlistment, singing, and you are given a fine practitioner's absence, you are a purpose surrounded by chance, a hole in chance. You can feel the clouds move over the sun from here. You can hear the sun return and the insect-hum spray up. You can lie still and feel this is the ultimate price. You feel it getting paid. By you. It is you.

MOTHER'S HANDS DRAWING ME

Dying only mother's hands continue
         undying, blading into air,
impersonal, forced, curving it
         down—drought incessant rain
revolution and the organs shutting
         down but not these extremities,
here since I first opened my first
eyes first day and there they were,
delicate, pointing, will not back off,
cannot be remembered. Mother,
         dying—mother not wanting to
         die—mother scared awakening
each night thinking she's dead—
         crying out—mother not
remembering who I am as I run
in—who am I—mother we must
take away the phone because who
will you call next—now saying I
dreamt I have to get this dress on, if
I get this dress on I will not die—
mother who cannot get the dress on
because of broken hip and broken
arm and tubes and coils and pan
and everywhere pain, wandering
delirium, in the fetid shadow-
         world—geotrauma—trans-
natural—what is this message

you have been scribbling all your
life to me, what is this you drag
again today into non-being. Draw it.
The *me* who is not here. Who is the
ghost in this room. What am I that
is now drawn. Where are we
heading. Into what do you throw
me with your quick eye—up onto
me then down onto the blank of the
page. You rip the face
off. I see my elbow there where
now you bend it with the pen, you
fill it in, you slough it off me onto
more just-now making of more
future. You look back up, you take
my strangeness from me, you
machine me, you hatch me in. To
make what, mother, here in this
eternity this second this million
years where I watch as each thing is
seen and canceled-out and re-
produced—multiplying aspects of
light in the morning air—the
fingers dipping frantic into the bag
of pens, pencils, then here they
are—the images—and the hands
move—they are making a
line now, it is our world,
it horizons, we ghost, we sleepwalk,
everything around us is leveled,
canceled, we background, we
are barely remains, we remain, but
for what, the fingers are deepening

curling, bringing it round, the mind
does not—I don't think—know this
but the fingers, oh, for all my life
scribbling open the unseen,
done with mere things, not
interested in appraisal, just
seizure—what is meant by
seizure—all energy, business-
serious, about direction, tracing
things that dissolve from thingness
into in-betweens—here firm lines,
here powdery lift off—hunger,
fear—the study begins—all is not
lost—the thought a few seconds
wide—the perusal having gone
from here to here, aggregates,
thicket, this spot could be where
we came in, or where we are saved,
could be a mistake, looks across
room through me, me not here
then, me trying to rise in the beam,
nothing I do will make it
happen, rock-face, work that
excludes everything that is not
itself, all urge in the process of
becoming all effect, how can I touch
that hand like snow moving, when
is it time again as here there is no
time, or time has been loaded but
not cocked, so is held in reserve, all
wound up, I was also made but not
like this, I look for reluctance,
expectation, but those are not the

temperatures—if only I could be in
the scene—my time is not
passing—whose is the time that is
passing—the hands rushing across
the paper, cloudy with a sun
outside also rushing scribbling—
wisdom turning itself away from
wisdom to be—what—a thing that
would gold-up but cannot, a patch
of blue outside suddenly like the
cessation of language when lips
cease to move—sun—self-
pronouncing—I want this to not be
my writing of it, want my hands not
to be here also, mingling with hers
who will not take my hand ever into
hers, no matter how late we are, no
matter that we have to run so fast
through all these people and I need
the hand, somewhere a radiant
clearing, are we heading for it, head
down towards the wide page, hand
full of high feeling, cannot tell if it
takes or gives, cannot tell what it is
that is generating the line, it comes
from the long fingers but is not
them, all is being spent, the feeling
that all—all that we need or have—
would be spent for this next thing,
this capture, actually loud though
all you can hear is the small
scratching, and I feel dusk
approaching though it is still early

afternoon, just slipping,
no one here to see this but me, told
loud in silence by arcs, contours,
swell of wind, billowing, fluent—
ink chalk charcoal—sweeps, spirals,
the river that goes
nowhere, that has survived the
astonishments and will never
venture close to that heat again, is
cool here, looking up at what,
looking back down, how is it
possible the world still exists, as it
begins to take form there, in the not
being, there is *once* then there is the
big vocabulary, loosed, like
a jay's song thrown down when the
bird goes away, cold mornings,
hauling dawn away with it, leaving
grackle and crow in sun—they have
known what to find in the unmade
undrawn unseen unmarked and
dragged it into here—that it be
visible.

Jorie Graham is the author of fourteen collections of poems. Her poetry has been widely translated and has been the recipient of numerous awards, among them the Pulitzer Prize, the Forward Prize, the Los Angeles Times Book Award, and the International Nonino Prize. She lives in Massachusetts and teaches at Harvard University.

More information is available at www.joriegraham.com.

This book was set in Bulmer with Bauer Bodoni titling and Times New Roman arrows.

Little Bears

THE PIRATE SUIT

Raewyn Caisley

Illustrated By Elise Hurst

rbP

Ragged Bears Publishing

RAGGED BEARS
Published by Ragged Bears Publishing Ltd.,
Unit 14A, Bennetts Field Industrial Estate,
Southgate Road,
Wincanton,
Somerset BA9 9DT, UK

First published 2011

1 3 5 7 9 10 8 6 4 2

A CIP catalogue record for this book is available from the
British Library

ISBN 978 1 85714 393 5

Printed in Poland

THE PIRATE SUIT

Ned's moved to a house by the sea with creaky stairs. And there's a smugglers' cove at the end of the lane. He'd like to be a pirate. His mum brings him long black boots, a pirate hat and a shiny silver cutlass. Dad makes his treehouse into a pirate ship. So when it's dark and the candlelight flickers in the windows, Captain Ned's adventure begins.

To the real Captain Ned
and his crew

Chapter One

As soon as they moved into the little house by the sea, with its creaky stairs and its far off view, Ned knew he was going to have to be a pirate. What else could you do with the smell of the ocean in your room, and a smugglers' cove at the end of the lane?

When Mum unpacked the dressing-up box Ned found his eye patch and scarf.

'I'm a pirate,' he growled to
Dad.

Dad chuckled and said, ' You
certainly are!'

When Aunty Zoe came to stay
Ned told her too.

'And if you don't do what I say,'

he added. 'I'll make you walk the plank!'

Aunty Zoe just smiled and shook her head. 'Your face looks like a storm at sea,' she said.

Whenever they went down
to the cove Ned dragged Dad's
heavy spade along. It would
make a proper clunk when it hit
the treasure chest.

'Careful you don't cut your toes
off with that,' said Mum.

In the evening he lay in bed and listened to the waves while Dad read him his pirate book, and every morning he checked the wind just like a real pirate would. But after a while it wasn't enough.

He never found any buried
treasure at the cove, and anyone
could have an eye patch and a
silly scarf.

'What's the matter?' Mum
asked when he threw the eye
patch and scarf back in the
dressing-up box one day.

Ned flopped down on the

settee in the conservatory. Mum
just looked at him and smiled.

'You're not the only one with
pirate blood in their veins,' she
said.

Ned didn't really know what
Mum meant, but he had a feeling
it was something good.

Chapter Two

Mum's new job was at
Winnacott's Garden Nursery. She
was going to teach people how
to make frog
ponds from old
tyres and paint
'Wacky Wellies' to sell
in the nursery shop.
Dad was going to
make things to sell
there too. He planned to build
garden statues from bits of rusty

machines and make 'Crazy
Creatures' out of crooked spoons
and wire.

Mum had something in her
bag when Dad and Ned went

to pick her up from work one
afternoon.

'What's that?' Ned asked.

'You'll have to wait until we get
home,' Mum said.

Aunty Zoe was waiting on the steps when they got home. She had something in a bag as well.

'Everyone's put a lot of work into this,' said Dad.

Dad let them in and then he went into the kitchen to start the tea. Mum and Aunty Zoe put their bags on the kitchen table.

Aunty Zoe was smiling. 'Go on,' she said.

Ned tipped the bags up and out tumbled a pair of long, black boots, a proper hat, and the most amazing pirate jacket he'd ever

seen.

'And that's not all,' said Dad.

He put the potato peeler down
and from behind his back he
pulled out a shining, silver

cutlass. Then he proudly held up
a wide leather belt, with a metal
buckle the size of a playing
card.

Chapter Three

Aunty Zoe helped Ned put the
jacket on. It was the colour of
blood with swirls of golden braid.
There were six shiny buttons
down the front. Ned put the boots
on next, then Dad made a hole
in the belt so that it would fit just
right. Once Ned had everything
on he felt a bit taller, and the

cutlass made him feel dangerous.

He ate his tea standing up, stabbing his mashed potato and slicing up his carrots. It was fun, but then he started to think. The kitchen wasn't really the place for a pirate. An idea burst into his

mind like cannon fire.

'Can we go down to the cove later on, Dad?' he asked.

Dad grinned. 'I'll take the dog for a run.'

While Dad threw a tennis ball for Grif, Ned climbed up on the rocks. There was a pointy rock that could have been the bow of a ship, and two enormous clouds overhead that looked like sails. A salty breeze blew in from the sea.

'Are you all right up there?' Dad called out.

Ned nodded. It was much better

now.

He sailed on and on into the setting sun, but after a while something started to feel wrong again.

'Woof!' went Grif. Ned looked down. Grif wanted him to come and play ...

That was it! Ned suddenly knew what the matter was! He didn't have any crew!

Dad called out again. It was time to go. Ned frowned

as he climbed down off the rocks.

'I know someone who's had a big day,' Dad said as they walked back up the lane.

Ned's eyes felt like they had sand in them.

When they got home Dad ran a bath, then he helped Ned put his pyjamas on.

'Not even pirates wear their boots to bed,' he said.

Chapter Four

As soon as he woke up the next morning Ned put his pirate suit back on. He wasn't as happy as he'd been when he first got it, but it was still the best thing he'd ever owned.

He checked the wind and went to find Dad. He was having a cup of coffee in the kitchen.

'Do you want to wear your pirate suit to school today?' Dad

asked when he saw Ned. 'I don't think Mrs Button would mind.'

Ned just stood in the kitchen doorway and grinned.

When they got to school he ran through the gates and went straight to his classroom.

'Well, who do have we here?' Mrs Button asked. 'Do I have to call you Captain Ned today?'

Ned just smiled and nodded his head.

At lunchtime Ned was the first one in the playground. He had a plan! The jungle gym under the

34

oak tree looked just like a sailing ship. He climbed on board and took the wheel. The wind was blowing from the east …

Soon Ned had more crew than he could count! Everyone who saw what he was doing wanted to join in.

'Set the sails!' he ordered his classmates. 'Fire the cannons! Hoist the Jolly Roger!'

They played pirates for the whole lunchbreak, but then the bell rang. Ned felt his heart drop down into his boots. He didn't

want it to be over yet.

'Why don't you take your jacket off,' Mrs Button said when he went inside. 'You can have a turn on the computer if you like.'

Ned looked sadly around the room. He couldn't do that.

'Oh well,' Mrs Button said. 'It is a magnificent thing. How about wearing it until hometime. But on Monday can you just be Ned again?'

Chapter Five

On Saturday morning Ned
flopped out of bed. He put his
pirate suit on, but he didn't
bother to check the wind. He
didn't worry about doing his
jacket up either. And he didn't

play any pirate games until late in the afternoon.

When Dad saw him in his treehouse he brought him out a glass of apple juice and a piece of cake. Dad had made the treehouse after they'd moved

in, and yesterday he'd nailed a steering wheel up so Ned could pretend it was a sailing ship. Today Dad had a cardboard tube under one arm.

'So you can watch out for Scurvy Dogs,' he said.

After they'd shared the cake and the apple juice, Dad turned to Ned.

'What's the matter, me heartie?' he asked. 'You look like your ship's run aground.'

Ned tried to smile but it was hard. Dad gave him a look like he understood.

'Hey!' he suddenly said.
'How about having tea up here
tonight?'

Ned instantly forgot all about being sad. Dad always had the best ideas!

Dad served tea as soon as Mum got home and they ate their sausages together in the treehouse.

Later on Mum lit tiny candles all around the garden. Dad fetched Ned's sleeping bag and pillow, and passed them up.

'Just in case you fall asleep,' he said.

'Do I have to wear my

pyjamas?' Ned asked. 'No, matie. Not right now,' smiled Dad.

Dad helped Ned pull his boots off, then Ned climbed into his sleeping bag and listened while Mum and Dad talked quietly down in the garden.

The feather on his hat nodded and swayed in the breeze. He loved his pirate suit more than anything, but somehow looking at the feather made him sad again.

It had been wonderful wearing his pirate suit to

school, but it was only once. If
only he could have had one really
proper pirate adventure. One
that matched how he felt when
he was wearing his suit.

'Sounds like a high tide tonight,'
Dad was saying to Mum.

Down in the cove the waves
rumbled like drums.

Chapter Six

Suddenly candle light flickered
in the treehouse window. 'Are
you asleep, Captain Ned?'
came a growly voice. 'No,' Ned
whispered. 'Good!' said the voice.
'You're needed on deck. The look
out's spied the Scurvy Dogs!'

Ned peered into the darkness,
and what he saw made him
almost fall out of the treehouse!
Mum, Dad and Aunty Zoe were
standing in the garden, and they

were all dressed up like pirates!
He could feel his heart beating
through his teeth.

'What are your orders, Captain
Ned?' Mum asked with a smile.
She had her stripy scarf around
her head, and an enormous gold

earring in one ear. Ned didn't know what to say.

'I think we'd better load the cannons,' said Dad.

Ned looked at him and beamed.

While Mum, Dad and Aunty Zoe gathered up all the tennis balls they could find, Ned climbed out of his sleeping bag

and grabbed his hat. He was as excited as he'd been the first time he went to the movies.

He was a bit scared too, but that was all right. Pirate adventures weren't meant to be too safe.

As he pulled on his boots Ned looked around the garden. The lawn was like the sea at night. Everything was black and the bushes bobbed like waves. When he was ready he stood up and took the wheel.

'Ahoy, Captain Ned!' Dad

called out, and his eyes were
sparkling in the dark.

Chapter Seven

Mum, Dad, Aunty Zoe and Ned
had the most magnificent pirate
adventure ever. They fired the
tennis balls onto the roof of the
house. *'Boom! Bang! Crash!'* 'Take
that you bunch of yellow bones!'
Mum cried.

Aunty Zoe had to shut Grif in
the potting shed for a while. 'Poor
old neighbours,' she said. 'They'll
think they're being attacked.'

Once they'd driven off the
Scurvy Dogs, they went on a
night-time treasure hunt.

'Here you go, Captain, Sir,'
Mum said, handing Ned a
marmite jar. It had a candle in
the bottom that smoked and
danced.

Like smugglers, they searched
the dark corners of the garden.

'Ah, ha!' Dad suddenly cried,
and Ned got such a fright it felt

like his skin had turned inside
out! When Mum held her candle
up, Dad was holding a bag of
chocolate coins.

After they'd found all the
treasure they could, they went
back to the treehouse to divide it
up. Dad told them stories of the
sea.

'Did I ever tell you about the time I wrestled a shark with me bare hands?' he asked.

Aunty Zoe slid a pile of coins across the floor to Ned. He grinned at Dad and shook his head.

'What about the time I saw a real live mermaid?' Dad said. 'She stole my heart.'

Dad smiled at Mum, and Ned loved it.

He knew Dad was making the stories up, but it didn't matter. Pirates were meant to tell tall tales.

Chapter Eight

Ned stayed up longer than ever before, but after a while he started to feel tired.

'What's our new heading, Captain Ned?' Dad growled.

'Just be Dad now, okay?' he said.

'Time for bed, is it?' Dad asked.

Dad picked up a candle and took Ned inside. He helped him put his pyjamas on, then he tucked him in and gave him a prickly-whisker kiss.

'So. Was that good fun?' Dad asked.

Ned grinned at Dad through halfshut eyes.

'Did you really wrestle a shark?' he asked.

'Cross me toes and fingers,' Dad growled.

Ned lay awake long after Dad had gone, listening to the waves crashing in the cove.

The golden braid on his jacket sparkled in the moonlight. Being a pirate had turned out

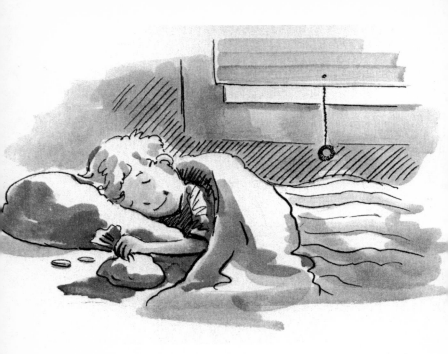

to be better than he could have imagined. But only because he had the best family to ever sail the seven seas...

Rigging

Fore
Mast

Sails

Figurehead

Anchor

Prow (front)

Cannons

Fore
(front)

Main Mast

Crows Nest

Mizzen Mast

The Helm or Ship's Steering Wheel

Poop Deck

The Main Deck

Jolly Roger

Captain's Cabin

Rudder

Starboard (right)

Aft (back)

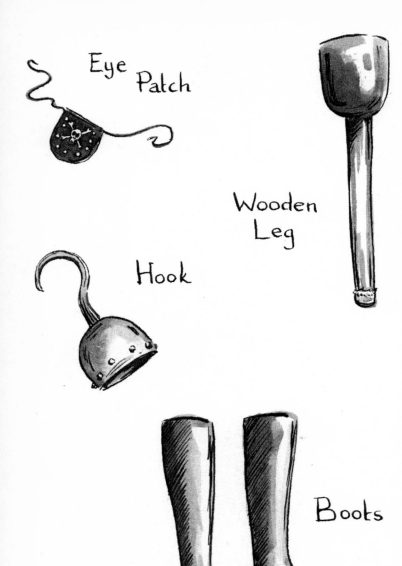

Eye Patch

Wooden Leg

Hook

Boots

Pirate Head
Scarf

Belt

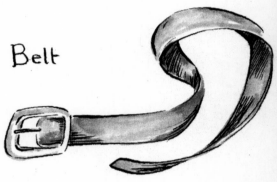

Captain's Hat

Pirate
Parrot

Pieces
of
Eight

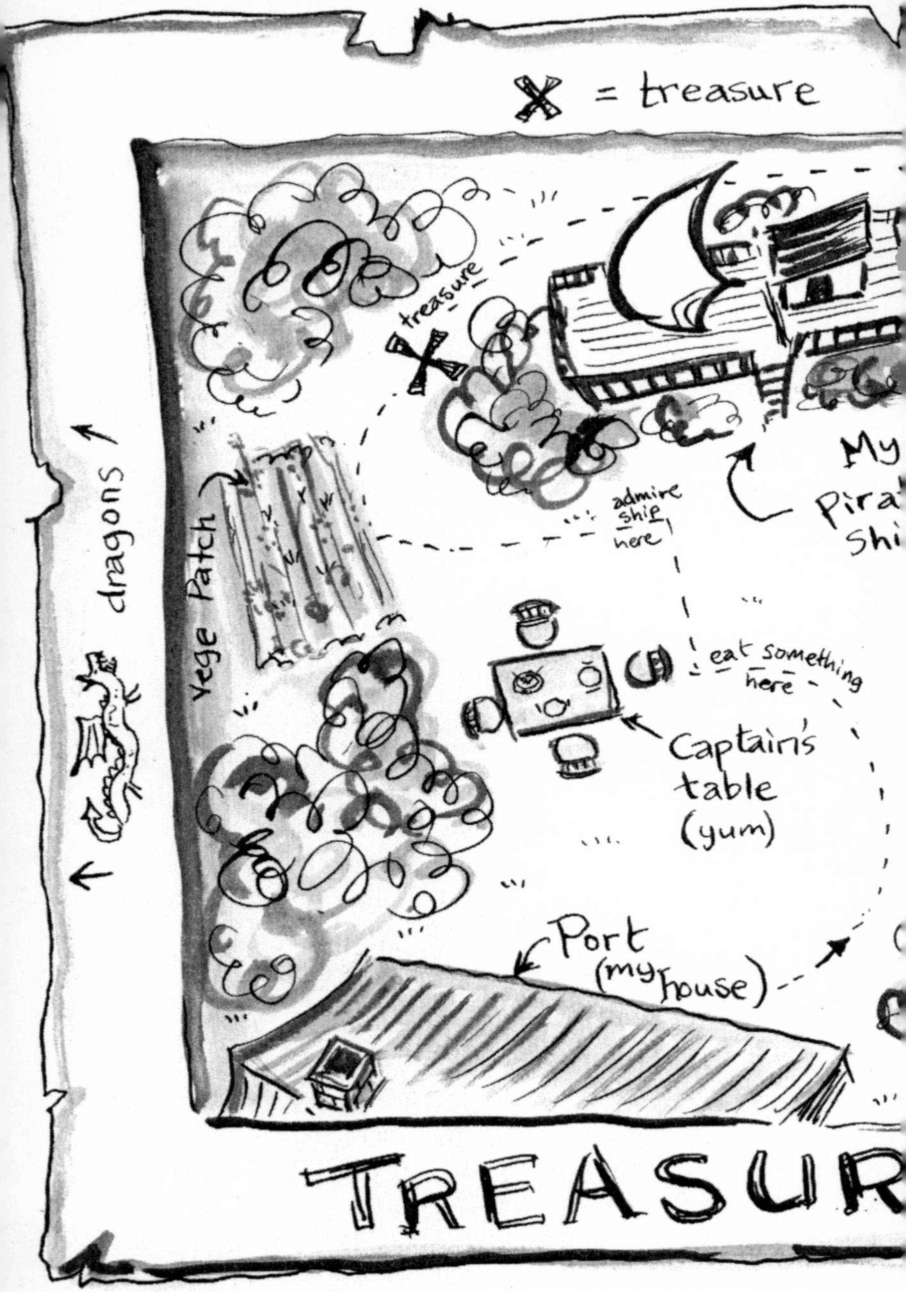

X = treasure
treasure
admire ship here
Vege Patch
My Pira Shi
dragons
eat something here
Captain's table (yum)
Port (my house)
TREASUR

the parrot ate this bit
treasure
(old tree stump)
Dead Man's Bluff
the Neighbours)
(Neighbours)
Scurvy Dogs!
sneak here
KEEP AWAY!
Hideout!
(Potting shed)
treasure
row boat
(wheelbarrow)
E MAP

RAEWYN CAISLEY

I once wrote a story about a little girl whose mother made her a flashing, sequinned mermaid's tail but I noticed that not a lot of boys were reading it! As I had a son of my own I knew that one day I would have to write a 'boy' version of the story for him but I didn't know what it was going to be about. Then when Jack started at pre-school he made a most remarkable new friend.

Can you imagine going to pre-school with a boy who thinks he is Captain Jack Sparrow? I met my son's new friend, 'Captain' Ned the day his dad was nailing a ship's wheel up in his treehouse. He'd got it for his birthday.

These days Ned prefers purple top hats to pirate suits and this year's birthday present was a garden gnome. I am quite sure this boy is going to provide me with plenty more great stories!

Raewyn Caisley trained as a primary school teacher. She has now written around twenty books for children, including *The Little Penguin* and *The Mermaid's Tail* (published in Happy Cat First Readers).

Elise Hurst has illustrated 50 books, many of them prize-winning picture books, and is a talented and versatile artist living in Australia.

REFUGEES AND PRIMARY CARE

Participative Development in General Practice

Penny Trafford and Fedelma Winkler

Published by
The Royal College of General Practitioners
2000

302603819W

The Royal College of General Practitioners was founded in 1952 with this object:

> *"To encourage, foster and maintain the highest possible standards in general practice and for that purpose to take or join with others in taking steps consistent with the charitable nature of that object which may assist towards the same."*

Among its responsibilities under its Royal Charter the College is entitled to:

> *"Diffuse information on all matters affecting general practice and issue such publications as may assist the object of the College."*

© Royal College of General Practitioners

First impression 2000

Published by the Royal College of General Practitioners
14 Princes Gate
Hyde Park
London, SW7 1PU

Designed by Book Production Consultants
Typeset, printed and bound in England by RPM Reprographics
Cover images courtesy of The Image Bank
ISBN 0 85084 258 1